THE
IRISH
SONGBOOK

COLLECTED, ADAPTED, WRITTEN, AND SUNG BY

THE CLANCY BROTHERS
AND
TOMMY MAKEM

ARRANGED FOR PIANO AND GUITAR BY

Robert DeCormier

COMPILED AND EDITED BY

Joy Graeme

WITH A FOREWORD BY

Pete Hamill

Oak Publications

New York   London   Sydney

Order No. OK 64188
US International Standard Book Number: 0.8256.2007.4
UK International Standard Book Number: 0.86001.280.8
Library of Congress Catalog Card Number: 78-80299

Exclusive Distributors:
Music Sales Corporation
225 Park Avenue South, New York, NY 10003 USA
Music Sales Limited
8/9 Frith Street, London W1V 5TZ England
Music Sales Pty. Limited
120 Rothschild Street, Rosebery, Sydney, NSW 2018, Australia

This edition is reprinted by arrangement
with Macmillan Publishing Co., Inc.

Printed in the United States of America by
Victor Graphics

THE PHOTOGRAPHS

2. The Clancy Brothers and Tommy Makem—*David Gahr.* 9. The Clancy Brothers and Tommy Makem—*C.B.S. Records.* 16. Robert Clancy's wedding party—*Independent Newspapers, Ltd., Dublin.* 38. Pat Clancy. 42. Mrs. Clancy. 57. Tommy Makem—*C.B.S. Records.* 58. Brendan Behan—*Photoworld, Inc.* 64. Tom Clancy and Helen Hayes—*Fred Fehl.* 68. Tom Clancy. 72. Tommy Makem. 77. Clancy Children—*Robert Clancy.* 83. Clancy Children. 86. Liam Clancy. 87. Clancy Children—*Robert Clancy.* 94. Pat Clancy—*C.B.S. Records.* 95. Tom Clancy—*C.B.S. Records.* 96. Liam Clancy—*C.B.S. Records.* 97. Tommy Makem—*C.B.S. Records.* 102. Master McGrath Monument—*Joy Graeme.* 108. The Clancy Brothers and Tommy Makem—*C.B.S. Records.* 114. Pat Clancy—*David Gahr.* 125. Liam Clancy—*David Gahr.* 126. Peg Clancy and Robert Clancy. 150. Tommy Makem—*David Gahr.* 156. Pat Clancy. 164. Sarah Makem—*Tommy Makem.* 167. Liam Clancy and Joe Heaney—*David Gahr.* 173. Mr. and Mrs. Clancy. 175. The Clancy Brothers and Tommy Makem—*C.B.S. Records.* 178-179. Eamon de Valera with The Clancy Brothers and Tommy Makem. 184. The Clancy Brothers and Tommy Makem—*David Gahr.*

Illustrations from the collections of the New York Public Library and the Library of Congress.

Foreword

I do most of my drinking in a small, dark saloon in Greenwich Village, a sweet, safe place most liberally stocked with beer and whiskey, with poets and sea captains, with newspapers and itinerant carpenters, with an occasional prizefighter or a visitor from Israel, bartenders from Boston and young ladies from everywhere else. The bar, which I shall not name, has a single function: to protect its clientele from the sorrows of the night; it takes that function seriously. It was in this saloon that I first met the Clancy Brothers and Tommy Makem.

It was on an evening dark with winter, with a harsh wind blowing through the streets of New York. The newspapers (I worked on one then) were carrying their usual cargo of disaster, violence, war and despair; it was obviously a night for drinking, and around midnight I dropped into my saloon on Sheridan Square. It was like walking into an explosion. I don't know why it happened that way, but all of them were there: Pat, Tom and Liam Clancy, and Tommy Makem, and they had commandeered the big round table in the back room, with about seventy people around them, and the great little waitresses running back and forth to the bar with trayloads of drinks, and the whole place was singing. The song was "The Leaving of Liverpool," which was one of their big hits that year, and they moved on to "Foggy Dew" and "Eileen Aroon" and "Isn't It Grand, Boys?" and "Rocks of Bawn" and a lot of other songs that are in this book. The voices were a shout, a lament, a challenge, a vow, all wrapped into one. Out beyond the confines of the saloon there were people still wrapped in the normal cloak of unhappiness. But inside, in the warmth, around the big table, these four splendid Irishmen and their accomplices banished that normal condition, at least for the duration of the evening. At four in the morning, when the place finally closed, we were all still singing. It was a beautiful evening.

We've seen a lot of each other in the years since, and for me New York is never quite New York anymore when The Boys, as they are called around the saloon, are out of town. On a gray winter's afternoon it is a comfort to know that Tom Clancy will be standing at the bar, drinking an Irish and milk if the previous evening had been bad, or a bloody Mary if it had been a disaster. It is a comfort because saloons and pubs are always family places when they are any good, and an afternoon with Tom is like an afternoon with a beloved brother, made especially pleasurable because this brother cares for the sounds and splendors of the English language.

So you can be there with Tom, who might be dressed in cowboy boots he once bought in Juarez, with his rough workingman's face breaking into laughter, or going hard and implacable at the thought of some further evidence of the injustice of the world, and he can break into a speech from Shakespeare to illustrate his point, or call forth an impeccable rendition of something by Dylan Thomas, or remember something said by an old friend like Brendan Behan, or talk with insight and erudition about the work of Eugene O'Neill; and since Tom is one of the least pompous men I know and is not given to holding mere literary seminars, he might go on to describe the perfidy of politicians he knows, the charms—or lack of them—of various women, the problems of drinking in New Zealand, some distant exploit of his or Pat's in the RAF during the Second World War, the personal life and paternity of foremen in Cleveland automobile plants, and the weather in Toronto.

Later in the afternoon, Pat Clancy will usually arrive, thinner, with clean, classic Irish features, wearing a good tweed Cork hat, a quick smile, the soft-voiced quiet man, the perfect Irishman to play Patrick Pearse if they ever made a film about the scholar-poet who helped liberate the GPO in 1916. Pat will order a Guinness, and talk will flow on. There was the time when Pat worked as an insurance man in Cleveland, the slums of Hough, and when the black ghetto of that city went up in flames his first instinct was to think of how desperate the country had become and then how much it would cost the insurance companies.

Some afternoons, especially if they are working that night somewhere, Tommy Makem comes around. Tommy is a member of the Pioneers, a movement of about 500,000 people who abstain from drinking liquor. So he usually arrives for dinner and coffee and an occasional ginger ale. He doesn't seem to need the drink to enjoy himself and often he will stay into the long loud night, singing in his pure clear voice, telling stories, laughing, and sharing the delights and disappointments of his fellow travelers.

It was an odd set of circumstances that brought them together. The Clancys were born in Carrick-on-Suir, a small, neat market town in County Tipperary. There were nine children in the family, which was headed by a father who loved opera and a mother who had spent her childhood in a pub called McGrath's, which her mother ran. Carrick these days is sharing some of Ireland's new prosperity, but it was not always that way, and the Clancys have always worked for a living. Tom Clancy worked as a Shakespearean actor and then was a singer with Sean Healy's dance band in 1941. "My big number was 'Red Moon Over Havana,' and later I did a very good 'White

Christmas,' " Tom remembers. "You couldn't exactly say that traditional music was in very good shape." When World War II broke out in 1939, Tom and Pat joined the RAF, like so many of the "wild geese" before them, and were gone for years. By 1950, after various adventures which had included Pat's expedition to Venezuela to search for emeralds, they had emigrated to Canada. They worked for a while in Canada, and then made their way to Cleveland, Ohio, where they had relatives. They spent most of their time working days in an auto body plant, while Tom continued his acting in the evenings with the Cleveland Repertory Theater.

"We might have ended up in California, or stayed in Cleveland forever," Tom remembers, "if it weren't for the bloody car." Somewhere they had picked up a 1939 Plymouth, without fenders, "a car that looked like an alligator," in Tom's words, and at one point decided to seek their fortunes in the West. "We got about to Chicago and the differential fell out," says Tom. "So we decided we would never make it to the West and headed for New York instead."

In New York they found a splendid tavern called the White Horse, filled with old wood and much noise and a variety of painters, writers and poets (it was the favorite saloon of Dylan Thomas), and also found a way to live to the fullest in America. Tom and Pat became actors, taking part in one of the early O'Casey revivals at the Cherry Lane Theater of *The Plough and the Stars* and acting all over the off-Broadway scene; they also discovered folk-singing.

For a while they lived with three other young men over a bowling alley in Newark, across the Hudson River, and worked five days a week at the Hoffman Soda plant. "We lived for the weekends," Tom remembers. But by the time Liam emigrated in 1955, Tom was acting in television shows. Liam could play the guitar a bit and had done some singing with a group in Carrick. Liam met Tommy Makem through another accident. Jean Ritchie, one of the most industrious collectors of folk music, had been to Ireland and had spent some time with Sarah Makem, Tommy's mother, who knew a lot of old songs. Then a girl named Diane Hamilton, after a collecting expedition to Nova Scotia, decided to make a similar tour of Ireland, England and Wales. She was given the Clancy address by Pat Clancy, and she got Sarah Makem's address from Jean Ritchie. She went to the Clancy's first, met Liam and asked him to travel with her around Ireland. While Miss Hamilton was transcribing Mrs. Makem's songs, Liam and Tommy Makem became friends. In late 1955, they emigrated within weeks of each other.

Then another accident happened, this one with near-disastrous consequences. Tommy Makem had emigrated to Dover, New Hampshire, a town that contained a disproportionate number of people from his home town of Keady, in County Armagh. Dover had a large textile industry but Tommy went to work in a steel plant. One day his left hand was crushed by two tons of steel. While his hand was being treated he came to New York on a visit, ran into Liam again and they formed a duo; they were joined occasionally by Pat and Tom. About this time Pat Clancy was forming Tradition Records, so Pat, Tom, Liam and Tommy recorded their first record, an album of Irish rebellion songs entitled "The Rising of the Moon." They soon made a second album, this time of drinking songs.

"One fine morning three of us were out of work," Liam remembers, "and we decided, what the hell. Several people had been bugging us to form a group and play together. We talked Pat into closing the Tradition Records' office for a while, and we went out to Chicago for a six-week engagement at the Gate of Horn. We wore black suits, white shirts and ties, sitting on four stools. I had about four chords on the guitar then, and Tommy Makem still couldn't play the tin whistle because his hand wasn't fully healed, but Pat could play the harmonica. So we started off that first night with the first song, which was 'O'Donnell Abu.' I had the capo in the wrong position on the guitar, so right off we found ourselves somewhere in the high soprano range. There were about twelve people in the audience, and I realized my mistake and decided to try and bluff it and sing soprano like John Jacob Niles. Tom turned to me and said: 'You can keep goin' if you like, but I'm not singin' in *that* bloody key!' Well, this was our first song, and we were nervous as hell as you can imagine, but the audience broke down laughing, and we said, hell, and loosened the ties, and took off the jackets, and had a few drinks sent up to us, and started to recreate the atmosphere of the White Horse. The following night there was a bigger crowd in, and the night after it was bigger, and we were packed out from there on."

"That was the beginning of it," says Tom. "If that car hadn't broke down, if Tommy Makem hadn't had his hand mashed, if we hadn't all ended up out of work at the same time, it wouldn't have happened. And we had one more piece of luck. We were back in New York, playing at the Blue Angel, and one night in walks Jim Downey, who owns the restaurant, and Jack Dempsey, the old heavyweight champion. They had another man with them, and it turned out he was from the Ed Sullivan Show. A few weeks later we played Sullivan for the first time, and that made us, professionally and nationally. So no one can ever tell me there's no such thing as luck!"

The Clancy Brothers and Tommy Makem were something new, both in folk music and in Irish music. They didn't approach their material as if it were liturgical music, to be performed in cathedrals. They attacked it, they assaulted it, they shouted it out loud and strong or filled it with deep emotion, and they shot it through with a lusty ribald humor. But they were not playing stage Irishmen; there was nothing to suggest leprechauns or clay pipes; they did not sing "Danny Boy" or "Galway Bay," and this at first puzzled some of their Irish-American auditors. "I remember one night, real early, one Irish-American lady asking us why we didn't sing some Irish songs," Liam remembers. "They wanted Tom to sing 'Danny Boy,' and he had to explain that Danny Boy had been there and gone."

"There was even a problem in Ireland," Pat remembers. "When we were young, the big song was 'Kevin Barry,' and you would hear it everywhere, day and night, in the street, in the pubs, in front parlors. And I remember one day the old woman across the street saying to my mother, 'Tell me, Mrs. Clancy, what used they sing before "Kevin Barry"?' "

In one way, the advent of the Clancy Brothers and Tommy Makem was a major cultural event in Ireland. They became part of the vanguard of what became known as the Ballad Revival. That was the full-fledged rediscovery, especially by young Irishmen, of the old songs of Ireland. Or as Liam puts it: "The Ballad Revival means, in its baldest form, that it became respectable again for so-called respectable people to sing working-class songs." "A lot of the old songs had begun to disappear," Pat remembers. "Or, at the very best, to fade away from the consciousness of many Irishmen. The British, of course, hadn't encouraged them ever, but then, after 1921, there wasn't much of an enemy left. And then there was Irish respectability."

"The better families in a town then," said Liam, "say, by the 1940s, would have had a piano, and they'd be learning light opera and things like that. The comeallyes, as we called them, were often associated with things they didn't want to remember. For instance, my mother never wanted to hear about pubs again, after the hardships of running McGrath's, and a lot of these songs were associated with pubs. And being brought up in a pub, she associated these songs with drink and madmen and fighting. And after a night of drinking, the Black and Tans would be there, and after she'd ask them for payment, they'd say: 'Is it true your son Peter is out with the rebels, Mrs. McGrath? Is it true?' It was true all right and they never paid for the drink."

But by the late 1950s a new generation of young Irishmen had arrived, young people who were not directly connected to the struggles of 1916 or the trauma of the bloody civil war which followed independence. Many of them had grown up blaming the economic stagnation of the country on the 1916 Syndrome, and there were bitter complaints that if you were not the son of a man who had been in the GPO, you could not make it in Ireland. The young people attracted by the Left, or convinced that the socialists and poets who had fought the war for independence had been betrayed, saw nationalism and patriotism as the curse of Ireland, and many of them emigrated. But in an odd way, the Clancys and their contemporaries then did something that seldom happens in a country: they turned much of that feeling around by providing an alternative life style, one that spoke with affection of the Irish past but realized the bombast and the bragging that was built into that past, and therefore could never be the past's prisoner. The Boys gave them a style of Irishness that was no longer mock-reverent, that returned to the roots of the Irish character—

racy, open, hearty, no longer stifled by Victorian platitudes. Their medium was primarily music, but it was also their rough, masculine approach to their material. All over Ireland today (and even in the Irish-American pubs in New York and Boston) you can see groups singing like the Clancys, using the old songs, and even writing new songs in the old forms.

"They're writing some marvelous songs right now," Liam says. "Some of them are even better than some of the old ones. Every time we go home, we learn new ones.

"You could tell the whole story of Ireland in her songs, but it would be a kind of emotional history of Ireland, a reaction to the things that have happened to us and which we have done. The whole story is there, right there in the songs."

And that, I suppose, is the key to Irish songs and to the songs in this book. Here you can feel that whole bitter tapestry of Irish history, a past suspended in the moment, time frozen for the duration of a song, some final triumph of words or music that has endured longer than the oppressors whose vicious acts inspired so many of the songs themselves. Here in the bravado and the boasting and the sadness and the hard bold swagger is the memory of distant kings, of scholars in bucolic country centers, of stark towers where the monks fled to be safe from the first of Ireland's many invaders; that time of pre-Norman Ireland, almost before history, is here in the songs; and so is what came after: that long and terrible seven hundred years when the Irish were a people to whom things were done.

Those were the centuries when the British Raj in Ireland attempted the systematic destruction of the Irish language, Irish music, Irish songs, Irish poetry and literature. As far back as 1366, the British enacted the Statutes of Kilkenny, which among other things barred Irish poets and musicians from English households. Things were to get worse.

There was, for example, Oliver Cromwell, a seventeenth-century religious maniac who apparently thought that the Almighty had given him the right to murder. At the town of Drogheda, he slaughtered every man, woman and child in the town of three thousand, writing afterward: "It has pleased God to bless our endeavors at Drogheda. . . . I wish that all honest hearts may give the glory of this to God alone, to who indeed the praise of this mercy belongs."

Under Elizabeth I, 10,000,000 acres of the best Irish land were stolen from the Irish and given to Englishmen, or to Scottish Protestant settlers in the North. In the early eighteenth century, the Penal Laws were passed, and if you think the Irish still too frequently brood over old hurts, consider some of these "laws." Irish Catholics were not allowed to vote in their own country; they could not hold public office, or enter the military, or take jobs in the civil service, or work as lawyers or teachers. The Catholic schools were abolished. No Catholic was allowed to own a horse worth more than five pounds, and if a Protestant coveted his Catholic neighbor's horse, he was allowed under the law simply to take it, paying the five pounds maximum no matter what the value of the horse. But the worst of the Penal Laws was the one forbidding Irishmen from leaving their farms to one son. Under the law, the land had to be divided among all the sons, and the result was the utter destitution of much of the Irish countryside. Farms became smaller and smaller, increasingly devoted to mere subsistence farming of potatoes, while the Anglo-Irish Protestant Ascendancy built great mansions on their stolen land and plush Georgian houses in Dublin.

The result, of course, was the Great Famine of 1846-51. The famine followed a potato blight, which destroyed the entire potato crop three years in a row. More than half the population of 8,000,000 depended entirely on potatoes for food; when the potato died, so did rural Irishmen. The figures are cold enough: 1,500,000 peasants died and another 1,000,000 emigrated. The details were something else. Children walked the roads of Ireland, their bellies bursting with disease, their eyes hollow with starvation. Irish mothers were found with babies at their dry breasts, lying in fields, their mouths stained green from trying to eat enough grass to stay alive. The emigrants piled into filthy trans-atlantic ships for Boston and New York, were jammed into the holds, where men fought each other for the privilege of eating rats and sawdust. The slave stolen from Africa at least had the small advantage of being property; the Irishman fleeing the great hunger was worth nothing. And through it all, the great landlords of Ireland went about business as usual: exporting the beef, pork, lamb and grain that might have saved the starving Irish. It was a mass atrocity that no Irishman has ever forgiven. (I remember one New Year's Eve in Carrick, sitting with Tom and Pat Clancy and relatives and friends, watching a television show. The British cattle industry was being decimated by an outbreak of foot-and-mouth disease, and a young Irishman suggested that Irish farmers, in an act of Christian charity, help replace the British herds by sending free cattle to their fellow farmers across the Irish Sea. And someone in the Clancy living room said yes, and we'll hang a medallion around each head saying "1847, with love." There was dark laughter and darker songs.)

But through it all there was a sense of rebellion, a need for heroes, a championing of martyrs. Until the last great struggle, the Irish always lost, but in losing they seemed to add to the growing legend of defiance. Kelly, the boy from Killane, died in the rebellion of 1798. Young Roddy McCorley, who went to die on the bridge of Toome that day, was in the Ulster rebellion the same year. Bold Robert Emmett led a tiny band in a suicidal raid on Dublin Castle in 1803. When Tommy Makem sings so powerfully that "The West's Awake," he is singing of the Irish struggle in

Connaught, where there was for so many years a passive acceptance of British rule ("Alas and well may Erin weep, that Connaught lies in slumber sleep"), to be followed by a roaring challenge, the gauntlet thrown down: "The West's Awake! The West's Awake! Sing O, Hurrah, let England Quake!" (Is it any accident that this is reported to be the favorite song of Senator Eugene McCarthy?) Alexis de Tocqueville, who visited Ireland in 1835, said, after hearing tales of the times of Cromwell and William of Orange: "Whatever one does, the memory of the great persecutions is not forgotten, and who sows injustice must sooner or later reap the fruits."

In the end, the British finally were to reap the bitter fruits. A brave little band of poets and socialists stormed the General Post Office in Dublin on Easter Monday, 1916, and though they failed, before the year was out the first large hole had been blown through the ramparts of the British Empire. By 1921, after a murderous guerrilla war masterfully commanded by Michael Collins, Ireland found herself largely at peace and almost free at last.

All of that is in these songs, and so is the feeling of reconciliation that came in the years afterward. It is no accident either that The Boys sing songs from other countries, including England. "You know, from a distance of three thousand miles," Liam said one day, "a lot of the old grievances and animosities between the Irish, the English, the Welsh and the Scots which seemed so important and personal at home simply disappear. You can see it here in the bar. Any night you can see the English lads in here, the Welsh lads, the Scots lads, in for a song and a carry-on. And it happens that way wherever we go. It's a kind of international brotherhood. Or maybe an international conspiracy."

So this book is a songbook, but it is something more. It records tides of feeling: small joys, large pains, the love of women and weather and sea, hunger, despairs, defeat, the smell of the Irish countryside, and the great piled banks of cloud, under which all those young men dreamed for seven hundred years, dreamed in the silence that was turned into song. And through all the Irish songs an odd figure still moves, the figure that moves through the secret heart of everyone who has ever passed through the Irish experience. He is the unnamed hero of all the songs the Clancys sing. It is he who sings with compassion at the end of an evening, when the quiet strains of "The Parting Glass" are raised to say good night. He knows what war it was they speak of in "Johnny, I Hardly Knew Ye."

—PETE HAMILL

vi

Contents

Óró, Sé Do Bheatha 'Bhaile!

(OH-ROW, SHAY DHU VA-HA WAL-YEH)

Written by Padraic Pearse, one of the leaders of the Irish Rebellion of 1916,
"Oro, Welcome Home" was an invitation to all the Irishmen in Europe who
were fighting for the British Empire and the freedom of small nations to
come home and tackle the ancient foe on their own little island.

Adapted by Tom Clancy, Pat Clancy,
Liam Clancy, and Tommy Makem

2

2. Tá Gráinne Mhaol ag teacht thar sáile,
   Thaw Grawn-yee Wail egg chockth horr sawl-yeh,

   Óglaigh armtha léi mar gharda;
   Og-lig or-ram-ha lay maw gawr-dha;

   Gaeil iad féin 's ni Gaill ná Spáinnigh,
   Gwale eedh fain snee Guile naw Spawn-ig,

   'S cuirfid siad ruaig ar Ghallaibh.
   Squirr-hidh sheed roo-ig err Gool-iv.

   Chorus

3. A bhui le Ri na bhfeart go bhfeiceam,
   Av-wee lah Ree nah varth guh veck-im,

   Muna mbeam beo 'na dhiaidh ach seachtain,
   Mun-ah mem byoh nah yeeg ock shock-thin,

   Gráinne Mhaol agus mile gaiscioch
   Grawn-yee Wail ogg-us meel-eh gosh-kee-ock

   Ag fógairt fáin ar Ghallaibh.
   Egg foh-girth fawn err Gool-iv.

   Chorus

Hi for the Beggarman

This is a version of the very popular story of the beggarman who makes off with the daughter of the house and then turns out to be a lord or nobleman (as in "The Whistling Gypsy"). We got this from our sort of second mother, Annie Roche. Annie had a store of old traditional songs which she never considered of interest to anyone until the ballad revival of the 1960s made her rack her brain for half-forgotten songs she remembered her mother singing.

Words and music by Annie Roche

1. The night be-ing dark and ver-y cold, A wo-man took pit-y on a poor old soul. She took pit-y on a poor old soul and asked him to come in. With a too-roo, roo-roo, ran-tin hi, A too-roo, roo-roo,

2. He sat him down in a chim-ney nook; He hung his coat up-on a hook. He hung his coat up-on a hook and mer-ri-ly he did sing.

ran - tin hi, Too - roo, roo - roo, ran - tin hi, And hi for the beg - gar - man.

3. In the middle of the night the old woman rose;
She missed the beggarman and all his clothes.
She clapped and clapped and clapped again, says, "He has me daughter gone."
Chorus

4. Three long years have passed and gone,
When this old man came back again
Asking for a charity: "Would you lodge a beggarman?"

5. "I never lodged any but the one,
And with that one me daughter's gone,
With that one me daughter's gone, so merrily you may gang."
Chorus

6. "Would you like to see your daughter now,
With two babies on her knee,
With two babies on her knee and another coming on?

7. "For yonder she sits and yonder she stands,
The finest lady in all the land;
Servants there at her command since she went with the beggarman."
Chorus

The Holy Ground

This song is about a district in Cohb, County Cork, frequented by sailors. As they were leaving on their ships they would cry, "Fine girl you are," to the girls gathered on the quays.

Adapted by Pat Clancy, Tom Clancy, Liam Clancy, and Tommy Makem

Moderate tempo, with strength

1. Fare thee well, my love - ly Di - - nah, a
now the storm is rag - - ing and

thou - sand times a - dieu,_____ For we're goin' a -
we are far from shore,_____ And the good old

3. And soon the storm is over and we are safe and well;
We will go into a public house and we'll sit and drink our fill.
We will drink strong ale and porter and we'll make the rafters roar,
And when our money is all spent, we will go to sea once more.
(Fine girl you are!)
Chorus

Johnny Is a Roving Blade

Johnny was a hard-drinking, hard-wenching man, and no matter what happened to him, he was always happy.

Words and music by Tommy Makem

3. What will you do if your true love goes?
   Hey, ho, my Johnny.
   What will you do if your true love goes?
   Hey, my Johnny-O.
   What will you do if your true love goes?
   "Any other flower is sweet as a rose;
   Plenty more in the garden grows."
   Johnny is a roving blade.
   Chorus

4. What will you do when you come to die?
   Hey, ho, my Johnny.
   What will you do when you come to die?
   Hey, my Johnny-O.
   What will you do when you come to die?
   "Look St. Peter in the eye
   And tell him that I'm very dry."
   Johnny is a roving blade.
   Chorus

Ar Fol Lol Lol O

This is well-known in the Irish and Scots Gaelic, at least in chorus and tune.
The English version bears little relation to the original as we first heard it, and
although written in the early part of the century, it seems appropriate today.

Adapted by Archie Fisher, Pat Clancy, Tom Clancy,
Liam Clancy, and Tommy Makem

Fol lee___ fol o ho - ro, ar fol lol lol ay.___

1. There's lilt in the song I sing, there's
2. And wheth - er the blood be high - land,

laugh - ter and love,___ There's tang of the sea and blue from
low - land or no,___ And wheth - er the skin be black or

heav - en a - bove.___ Of rea - son there's none and why should there
white as the snow,___ Of kith and of kin we're one, be it

14

be ___ for bye, _____ As long as there's
right, be it wrong, _____ As long as our

fire in the blood and a light in the eye. ___ Ar fol lol lol
voi - ces join the cho - rus of song. ___

D. S.

Coda

lee ___ fol o ho - ro, ar fol lol lol ay. _____

15

I Once Loved a Lass

This is one of the most beautiful of Scottish love songs. The lines about strawberries growing in the salt sea and ships sailing in the forest refer to the impossible riddle of love.

Adapted by Pat Clancy, Tom Clancy,
Liam Clancy, and Tommy Makem

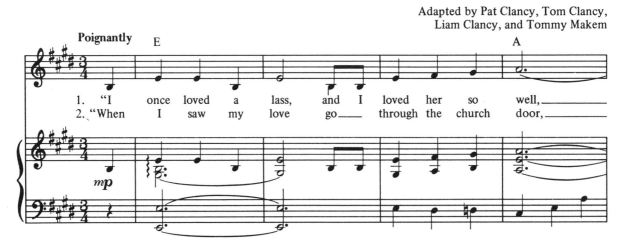

1. "I once loved a lass, and I loved her so well,_____
2. "When I saw my love go through the church door,_____

3. "When I saw my love a-sit down to dine,
   I sat down beside her and I poured out the wine;
   And I drank to the lass that should have been mine,
   But now she is wed to another.

5. "So dig me a grave and dig it so deep
   And cover it over with flowers so sweet;
   And I'll turn in for to take a long sleep,
   And maybe in time I'll forget her."

4. "The men of yon forest, they ask it of me,
   'How many strawberries grow in the salt sea?'
   And I ask of them back with a tear in my eye,
   'How many ships sail in the forest?'

6. So they dug him a grave and they dug it so deep;
   They covered it over with flowers so sweet.
   And he's turned in for to take a long sleep,
   And maybe by now he's forgotten.

Redmond O'Hanlon

Redmond O'Hanlon was a highwayman in the true Robin Hood spirit. He took from the rich and gave to the poor; his territory was South Armagh. Apparently he thought a lot of himself, for when holding up a coach, he would say to the passengers, "Come out and be robbed by the handsomest man in Ireland." Before turning highwayman he had earned the title of Papal Count; the Pope had bestowed the honor upon him for a very chivalrous deed he had performed during a great battle.

Words and music by Tommy Makem

1. There was a man lived in the North, a he-ro brave and bold, Who robbed the wealth-y land-lords of their sil-ver and their gold; He gave the mon-ey to the poor to pay their rent and fee, Count Red-mond O'-Han-lon, the

2. He had a no-ble big black horse that was his joy and pride, A brace of load-ed pis-tols that he car-ried by his side; He roamed the hills and val-leys with a spir-it wild and free, Count Red-mond O'-Han-lon, the

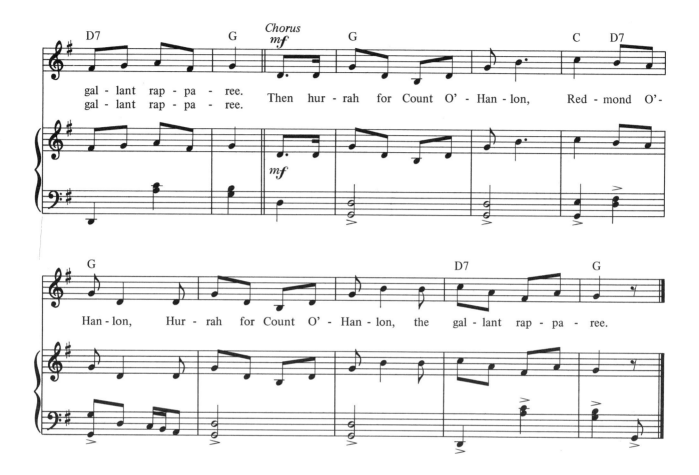

gal - lant rap - pa - ree.
gal - lant rap - pa - ree. Then hur - rah for Count O' - Han - lon, Red - mond O'-

Han - lon, Hur - rah for Count O' - Han - lon, the gal - lant rap - pa - ree.

3. 'Twas high upon Slieve Gullion that he used to ply his trade,
   And Squire Johnston from the Fews this handsome offer made:
   He said, "I'll give four hundred pounds to hang him from a tree."
   But not a man in all the land would sell the rapparee.
   Chorus

4. They sent the soldiers after him to try and bring him back;
   O'Hanlon only laughed at them upon the mountain track.
   And while the soldiers slept that night among the mountain gorse
   He stole their guns and rode away upon his noble horse.
   Chorus

5. 'Twas back in sixteen-eighty-one when Count O'Hanlon died,
   And still along Slieve Gullion's slopes they speak of him with pride.
   And anyone will tell you, from Rathfriland to Forkhill,
   That in the silence of the night you'll hear him riding still.
   Chorus

Éamann an Chnoic

(AY-MON A KUN-ICK)

Edmond O'Ryan, the hero of this Gaelic song, was born in Kilnamanagh, County Tipperary, before the wars of 1690. After the defeat of James II, whom he supported, he was outlawed and his estates confiscated. In this beautiful song, which he is supposed to have written, he comes to his sweetheart's door seeking shelter and tells of the hardships he is suffering.

Adapted by Pat Clancy, Tom Clancy,
Liam Clancy, and Tommy Makem

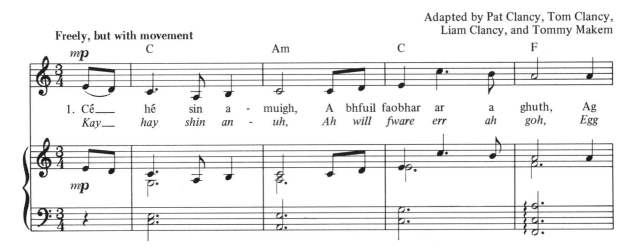

1. Cé___ hé sin a - muigh, A bhfuil faobhar ar a ghuth, Ag
Kay___ hay shin an - uh, Ah will fware err ah goh, Egg

21

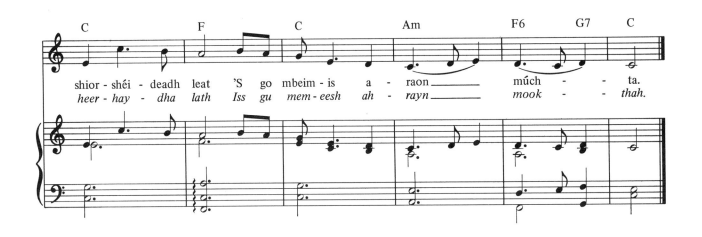

shior - shéi - deadh leat 'S go mbeim - is a - raon_____ múch - - ta.
heer - hay - dha lath Iss gu mem - eesh ah - rayn_____ mook - - thah.

2. Is fada mise amuigh
Iss fod-ha mish am-uh

Faoi shneachta is faoi shioc
Fwee nock-thes fwee huck

'S gan dánacht agam ar aon neach;
Sgon dhawn-ockt ah-gum err ain nock;

Mo sheireach gan scor,
Muh hesh-ruck gawn scur,

Mo bhranar gan chur,
Muh vron-ur gawn cur,

Is gan iad agam ar aon chor!
Iss gawn eedh ah-gum err ain cur!

Nil caraid agam
Neel kor-ah ah-gum

Is danaid liom san,
Iss dhun-ah lum sun,

Do ghlacfadh mé moch ná déanach,
Dhu glock-hug may muck naw day-nock,

'S go gcaithfidh mé dul
Sgu gay-ig may dhull

Thar farraige soir
Horr for-igg-ah sirr,

Ó is ann ná fuil aon de m' ghaoltaibh.
Os oun naw fwill ain them gwale-thiv.

Paddy Doyle's Boots

Paddy Doyle was a Liverpool-Irish boarding master. The song was sung in "bunting," or tying of a sail.

Adapted by Pat Clancy, Tom Clancy,
Liam Clancy, and Tommy Makem

3. To me way-ay-ay-ay ah!
   We'll all shave under the chin.

4. To me way-ay-ay-ay ah!
   We'll all throw mud at the cook.

5. To me way-ay-ay-ay ah!
   We'll pay Paddy Doyle for his boots.

What Would You Do
If You Married a Soldier?

These philosophical words were set to an old dance tune.

Adapted by Pat Clancy, Tom Clancy,
Liam Clancy, and Tommy Makem

24

did-dl-y da dum, A rout the da, doubt the da, did-dl-y da dum, Da da

did-dl-y da dum, Da dee da dum da did-dl-y da dee da did-dl-y da dum.

3. The praties are dry and the frost is all over;
   Kitty, lie over next to the wall.
   The summer is come and we're all in the clover;
   Kitty, lie over next to the wall.
   Chorus

4. Oh, what would you do if you married a soldier?
   "What would I do but to follow the gun?"
   And what would you do if he died in the ocean?
   "What would I do but to marry again?"
   Chorus

The Maid of the Sweet Brown Knowe

The "Knowe" mentioned in the title is a small hill or knoll. The song is a warning to all fair maids not to try and run their men's lives—especially before they have caught them!

Adapted by Tommy Makem

1. Oh, come, all you lads and lassies, And listen to me a-
2. Said he, "My pretty fair maid, Will you come along with

while, And I'll sing for you a verse or two That will cause you all to
me? We'll both go off together, And it's married we will

smile. It's all about a fair young man I'm going to tell you
be. We'll join our hands in wedlock bands I'm speaking to you

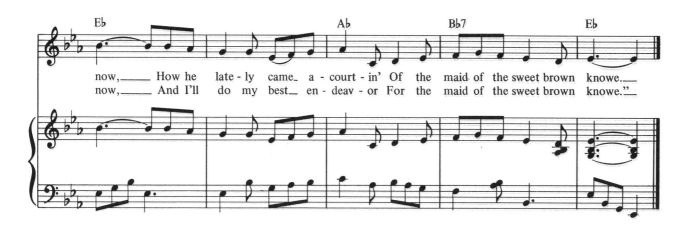

now,_____ How he late-ly came_ a-court-in' Of the maid of the sweet brown knowe._

now,_____ And I'll do my best_ en-deav-or For the maid of the sweet brown knowe."_

3. This fair and fickle young thing,
   She knew not what to say;
   Her eyes did shine like silver bright
   And merrily did play.
   She said, "Young man, your love's subdued,
   For I'm not ready now,
   And I'll spend another season
   At the foot of the sweet brown knowe."

4. Said he, "My pretty fair maid,
   How can you answer so?
   Look down on yonder valley
   Where my verdant crops do grow.
   Look down on yonder valley
   Where horses, men and plow
   Are at their daily labor
   For the maid of the sweet brown knowe."

5. "If they're at their daily labor,
   Kind sir, it is not for me,
   For I've heard of your behavior,
   For I have indeed," said she.
   "There is an inn where you call in,
   I've heard the people say,
   And you rap and you call and you pay for all
   And go home at the break of day."

6. "If I rap and I call and I pay for all,
   The money it is my own,
   And I'll never spend your fortune,
   For I hear that you have none.
   You thought you had my poor heart broke,
   Talking with me now,
   But I'll leave you where I found you:
   At the foot of the sweet brown knowe."

Galway City

The Galway version of "Spanish Lady," this is about a young lady who has great notions of "upperosity."

Adapted by Pat Clancy, Tom Clancy,
Liam Clancy, and Tommy Makem

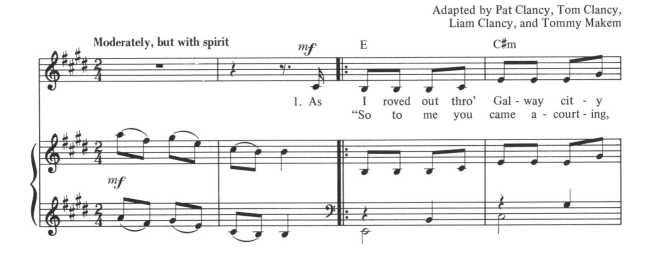

1. As I roved out thro' Gal - way cit - y
"So to me you came a - court - ing,

At the hour of twelve at night,
My kind fa-vours for to win;
Who should I see but a hand-some dam-sel,

Comb-ing her hair by can-dle-light.
If you nev-er did call a-gain.
"Las-sie, I have come a-court-in',
What would I do when I go walk-ing,

Your kind fa-vours for to win;
Walk-ing out in the morn-ing dew?
And if you'll but smile up-on me,
What would I do when I go walk-ing,

Chorus

Next Sun-day night I'll call a-gain."
Walk-ing out with a lad like you?"
Rad-dy a the too dum too dum too dum,

But 'twould give me the great-est plea-sure

29

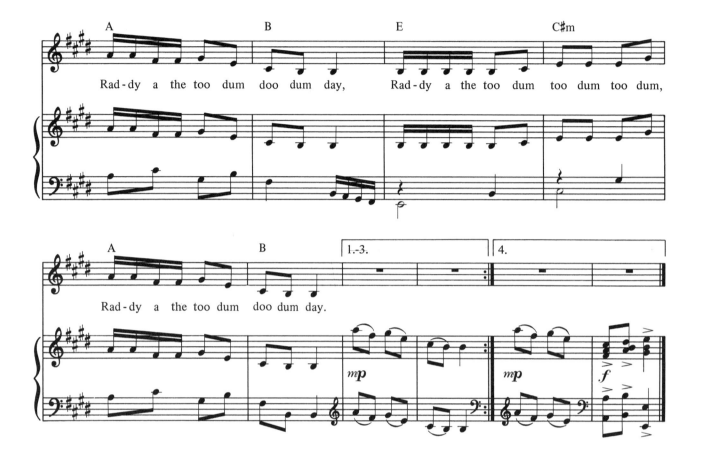

Rad - dy a the too dum doo dum day, Rad - dy a the too dum too dum too dum,

Rad - dy a the too dum doo dum day.

3. "Lassie, I have gold and silver;
   Lassie, I have houses and lands;
   Lassie, I have ships on the ocean;
   They'll be all at your command."
   "What do I care for your ships on the ocean?
   What do I care for your houses and lands?
   What do I care for your gold and silver?
   All I want is a handsome man."
   Chorus

4. "Did you ever see the grass in the morning
   All bedecked with jewels rare?
   Did you ever see a handsome lassie,
   Diamonds sparkling in her hair?
   Did you ever see a copper kettle
   Mended with an ould tin can?
   Did you ever see a handsome damsel
   Married off to an ugly man?"
   Chorus

Johnny, I Hardly Knew Ye

A bitter, savage comment by a woman who has lost most of her man, this
song dates back to the early nineteenth century, when the British Government recruited Irishmen for the East India Service.

Adapted by Pat Clancy, Tom Clancy,
Liam Clancy, and Tommy Makem

sweet A - thy, A stick in my hand and a drop in me eye, A dole - ful dam - sel
looked so mild, When my poor heart you first be-guiled? Why did ye ski - da - dle from

I heard cry: "John-ny, I hard - ly knew ye." "With your guns an' drums, an'
me an' the child? John-ny, I hard - ly knew ye."

Chorus

drums an' guns, hoo - roo_____ hoo - roo,_____ With your guns an' drums, an'

drums, an' guns hoo - roo_____ hoo - roo,_____ With your guns an' drums, an'

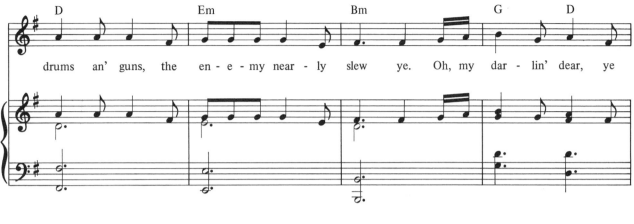

drums an' guns, the en-e-my near-ly slew ye. Oh, my dar-lin' dear, ye

look so queer; John-ny, I hard-ly knew ye."

3. "Where are the legs with which you run, hoo-roo hoo-roo,
   Where are the legs with which you run, hoo-roo hoo-roo,
   Where are the legs with which you run
   When first you went to carry a gun?
   Indeed, your dancing days are done.
   Johnny, I hardly knew ye."
   Chorus

4. "You haven't an arm, you haven't a leg, hoo-roo hoo-roo,
   You haven't an arm, you haven't a leg, hoo-roo hoo-roo,
   You haven't an arm, and you haven't a leg;
   You're an eyeless, boneless, chickenless egg.
   Johnny, I hardly knew ye."
   Chorus

5. "I'm happy for to see you home, hoo-roo hoo-roo,
   I'm happy for to see you home, hoo-roo hoo-roo,
   I'm happy for to see you home,
   All from the island of Ceylon,
   So long of flesh, so pale of bone.
   Johnny, I hardly knew ye."

Last Chorus:
"With your guns an' drums, an' drums an' guns, hoo-roo hoo-roo,
With your guns an' drums, an' drums an' guns, hoo-roo hoo-roo,
With your guns an' drums, an' drums an' guns, the enemy never slew ye.
Oh, my darlin' dear, you look so queer;
Johnny, I hardly knew ye."

My Son Ted

This is a version of "Mrs. McGrath," which in 1913-1916 was the most popular marching song of the Irish volunteers. It is probably the first antiwar song.

Adapted with new words by Joan Clancy

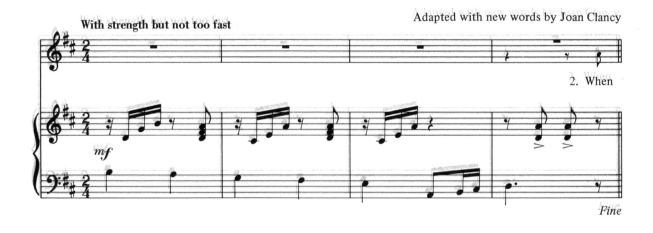

1. Mis - sus Mc-Grath lived near the sea - shore For the space of sev-en long years or more, When she
Ted he land - ed with-out an - y legs And in their place two wood-en pegs, And when

spied a ship com-ing in - to the bay: "This is my son Ted-dy; d' ye clear the way."
she kissed him a doz-en or two, Say-ing, "Blood, now, Ted, can this be you?"

Chorus

(Fine)
D. C.

Wish - a ring dong da, Ring-a dong-a-da, Ring dong dad-dy, Wish-a ring dong da.

3. "Oh Ted a graw, were you drunk or blind
When you left your two fine legs behind?
Or was it walking across the sea
You threw your two fine legs away?"
Chorus

5. "O Ted a graw, why weren't you cute
And run away from the Frenchman's shoot?
'Tisn't my son Ted is in it at all,
Because he'd run from a cannonball."
Chorus

4. "Oh, no, I was not drunk or blind
When I left my two fine legs behind.
But a cannonball in fourth of May
Swept my two fine legs away."
Chorus

6. "Now foreign wars I do proclaim
Between Don John and the king of Spain.
I'd rather have my Teddy as he used to be
Than the king of France and his whole navy."
Chorus

William Bloat

"To Hell with the Pope," "No Surrender," "Hang King Billy," are familiar slogans in Belfast, a city where Protestants and Catholics manage to live together leading highly Christian lives—hating each other passionately for the love of God. The song about William Bloat, a good Protestant, is really a commercial, one of the first elaborate commercials for an Irish product (non-alcoholic).

Words traditional
Music by Tommy Makem

1. In a mean a-bode on the
   he was glad he had

Shan-kill Road Lived a man named Wil-liam__ Bloat, And he
done what he had As she lay there stiff and__ still, 'Til

had a wife, the bane of his life, Who al-ways got his
sud-den-ly awe of the an-gry__ law Filled his soul with an aw-ful

goat.
And one day at dawn, with her night - dress on, He___
chill.
And to fin - ish the fun so___ well be - gun, He de-

slit her blood - y___ throat.
cid - ed him - self to kill.

1.-3.
2. Now,___ lin - en.___
3. Then he

4.

3. Then he took the sheet from his wife's cold feet,
   And he twisted it into a rope;
   And he hanged himself from the pantry shelf –
   'Twas an easy end, let's hope.
   With his dying breath and he facing death,
   He solemnly cursed the Pope.

4. But the strangest turn of the whole concern
   Is only just beginning;
   He went to hell, but his wife got well,
   And she's still alive and sinning.
   For the razor blade was German-made,
   But the rope was Belfast linen.

Mr. Moses Ri-Tooral-i-ay

At one time the Irish language, Gaelic, was forbidden by British law. This is a song about a Jewish merchant who arrived in a small town and opened a store, over which he put his name in Hebrew. A very ambitious British policeman came along, took one look at the Hebrew, assumed it was Gaelic, and dragged the Jew into court. That's the gist of it. It wasn't written so much to show the great love between the Irish and the Jews as to show the stupidity of the British.

Adapted by Pat Clancy, Tom Clancy
Liam Clancy, and Tommy Makem

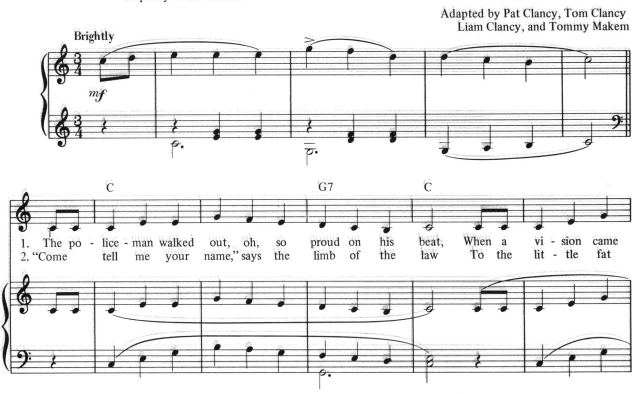

1. The po - lice - man walked out, oh, so proud on his beat, When a vi - sion came
2. "Come tell me your name," says the limb of the law To the lit - tle fat

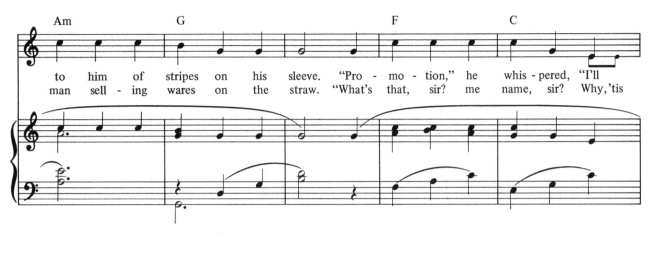

to him of stripes on his sleeve. "Pro - mo - tion," he whis - pered, "I'll
man sell - ing wares on the straw. "What's that, sir? me name, sir? Why, 'tis

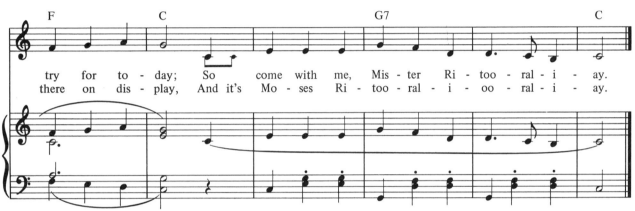

try for to - day; So come with me, Mis - ter Ri - too - ral - i - ay.
there on dis - play, And it's Mo - ses Ri - too - ral - i - oo - ral - i - ay.

3. Now, the trial it came on and it lasted a week.
   One judge said 'twas German; another, 'twas Greek.
   "Prove you're Irish," said the policeman, "and beyond it say nay;
   And we'll sit on it, Moses Ri-tooral-i-ay."

4. Now, the prisoner stepped up there as stiff as a crutch.
   "Are you Irish or English or German or Dutch?"
   "I'm a Jew, sir; I'm a Jew, sir, that came over to stay,
   And my name it is Moses Ri-tooral-i-ay."

5. "We're two of a kind," said the judge to the Jew;
   "You're a cousin of Briscoe and I am one too.
   This numbskull has blundered and for it will pay."
   "Wisha that's right," says Moses Ri-tooral-i-ay.

6. There's a garbage collector who works down our street;
   He once was a policeman, the pride of his beat.
   And he moans all the night and he groans all the day,
   Singing, "Moses Ri-tooral-i-ooral-i-ay."

The Black Cavalry

This concerns the hazards and fun of boarding houses in the last century.
The fleas ("black cavalry") have fun on the body of the boarder.

Adapted by Pat Clancy, Tom Clancy,
Liam Clancy, and Tommy Makem

1. In the first of me down-fall I put out the door,_____

And I straight made me way on for Car-rick-on-Suir,_____

Go-ing out by / Rath-ro-nan 'twas late in the

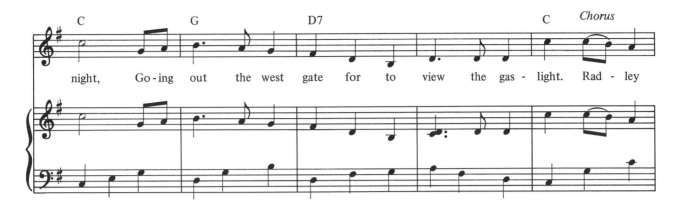

night, Go-ing out the west gate for to view the gas - light. Rad - ley

fal the did-dle - I, Rad - ley fal the did-dle ai - ro.

2. There I met with a youth and I unto him said,
   "Would you kindly direct me to where I'll get a bed?"
   It was then he directed me down to Cook's Lane,
   To where old Dick Darby kept an old sleeping cage.
   Chorus

3. Then I put up and down 'til I found out the door,
   And the missus came out and these words to me said,
   "If you give me three coppers I'll give you a bed."
   Chorus

4. She took me upstairs and she put out the light,
   And in less than five minutes I had to show fight.
   In less than five more sure the story was worse,
   For the fleas came about me and brought me a curse.
   Chorus

5. All round me body they formed an arch,
   And all round me body they played the dead march.
   The bloody old major gave me such a nip
   That he nearly had taken the use of me hip.
   Chorus

6. Now I'm going to me study, these lines to pen down,
   And if any poor traveller should e'er come to town,
   If any poor traveller be knighted like me,
   Oh, beware of Dick Darby and the black cavalry.
   Chorus

Eileen Aroon

In the original Gaelic version of this song there was a long tragic love story involved. In the later version written in English only the universal sentiments of love and change remain. Few finer verses have been written than that beginning, "Youth will in time decay."

Adapted by Pat Clancy, Tom Clancy,
Liam Clancy, and Tommy Makem

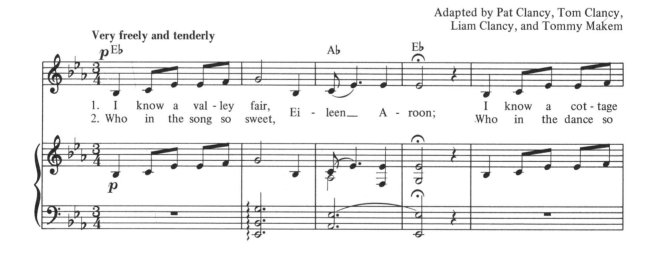

1. I know a val - ley fair, Ei - leen A - roon; I know a cot - tage
2. Who in the song so sweet, Ei - leen A - roon; Who in the dance so

there, Ei - leen___ A - roon, Far in the val - ley shade I know a ten - der
fleet, Dear are her charms to me, dear - er her laugh - ter

maid, Flow'r of___ the___ ha - zel glade, Ei - leen___ A - roon.
free, Dear - est___ her___ con - stan - cy, Ei - leen___ A - roon.

3. Were she no longer true, Eileen Aroon,
   What would her lover do, Eileen Aroon?
   Fly with a broken chain, far o'er the sounding main,
   Never to love again, Eileen Aroon.

4. Youth will in time decay, Eileen Aroon;
   Beauty must fade away, Eileen Aroon.
   Castles are sacked in war, chieftains are scattered far,
   Truth is a fixed star, Eileen Aroon.

As I Roved Out

"As I Roved Out" is a lovely beginning to any song. Like so many love songs
(the good old ones) you have to follow this closely to get the full measure.

Adapted by Sarah Makem, Pat Clancy, Tom Clancy,
Liam Clancy, and Tommy Makem

And she sang lilt-da-doo-dle, lilt-a-doo-dle, lilt-a-doo-dle-dee, And she

hi-da-land-da-dee, And she hi-da-land-da-dee, and she land - dae.

3. "What age are you, my nice sweet girl?
   What age are you, my honey?"
   How modestly she answered me,
   "I'll be sixteen age on Sunday."
   Chorus

4. I went to the house on the top of the hill
   When the moon was shining clearly;
   She arose to let me in,
   For her mammy chanced to hear her.
   Chorus

5. She caught her by the hair of the head,
   And down to the room she brought her;
   And with the root of a hazel twig,
   She was the well-beat daughter.
   Chorus

6. "Will you marry me now, my soldier lad?
   Marry me now or never?
   Will you marry me now, my soldier lad,
   For you see I'm done forever?"
   Chorus

7. "No, I won't marry you, my bonny wee girl,
   I won't marry you, my honey,
   For I have got a wife at home,
   And how could I disown her?"
   Chorus

8. A pint a night is my delight,
   And a gallon in the morning;
   The old women are my heartbreak,
   But the young ones is my darling.
   Chorus

Nell Flaherty's Drake

The main character of this anonymous nineteenth-century ballad is said to be a secret code name for Robert Emmet, an exceptionally charming youth who led a small uprising in Dublin in 1803, for which he was publicly hanged. Emmet's famous "speech from the dock," in which he requested that no epitaph for him be written until Ireland took her place among the nations of the earth, assures him of an eternal place in the hearts of all Irish nationalists.

Adapted by Pat Clancy, Tom Clancy,
Liam Clancy, and Tommy Makem

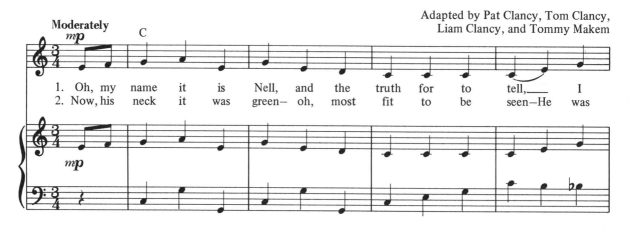

1. Oh, my name it is Nell, and the truth for to tell,—— I
2. Now, his neck it was green— oh, most fit to be seen—He was

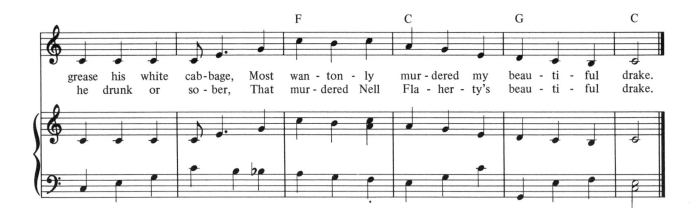

grease his white cab-bage, Most wan-ton-ly mur-dered my beau-ti-ful drake.
he drunk or so-ber, That mur-dered Nell Fla-her-ty's beau-ti-ful drake.

3. May his spade never dig, may his sow never pig,
   May each hair in his wig be well thrashed with a flail;
   May his door have no latch, may his roof have no thatch,
   May his turkeys not hatch, may the rats eat his meal.
   May every old fairy from Cork to Dunleary
   Dip him smug and airy in river or lake,
   That the eel and the trout, they may dine on the snout
   Of the monster that murdered Nell Flaherty's drake.

4. May his pig never grunt, may his cat never hunt,
   May a ghost ever haunt him at dead of the night;
   May his hens never lay, may his horse never neigh,
   May his goat fly away like an old paper kite.
   That the flies and the fleas may the wretch ever tease,
   May the piercing March breeze make him shiver and shake;
   May a lump of a stick raise the bumps fast and thick
   On the monster that murdered Nell Flaherty's drake.

5. Now the only good news that I have to infuse
   Is that old Paddy Hughes and young Anthony Blake,
   Also Johnny Dwyer and Corney Maguire,
   They each have a grandson of my darling drake.
   My treasure had dozens of nephews and cousins,
   And one I must get or my heart it will break;
   To set my mind aisy or else I'll run crazy –
   So ends the whole song of Nell Flaherty's drake.

ROBERT EMMET (1780−1803)

Ireland's Patriot Martyr

When my Country takes her place among the nations of the earth then and not till then let my Epitaph be written.

An Poc Ar Buile

(ON PUC ERR BWILL-A)

A joyous romp with a puck goat on the rampage. Neither a policeman nor a
priest can stop its mad career.

Words and music by Donal O'Mullain

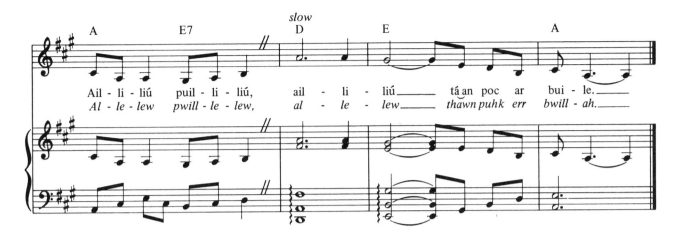

Ail - li - liú   puil - li - liú,   ail - li - liú_____ tá an poc ar   bui - le._____
Al - le - lew   pwill - le - lew,   al - le - lew_____ thawn puhk err   bwill - ah._____

2. Do ritheamar trasna   tri ruilleogach,
   Dhuh ri-hem-ur thras-nah three rill-oh-gock,

   Is do ghluais an comhrac ar fud na   muinge,
   Iss dhu gloosh on kohr-ick err fudh nah mwing-ah,

   Is treascairt da bhfuair sé sna   turtóga,
   Iss thras-kirt dhaw   voor shay snah thor-thohg-ah,

   Chuas ina ainneoin ar a dhroim le fuinneamh.
   Kyoos nan-yohn err ah grim lay fwinn-ev.

   Chorus

3. Nior fhag se carraig go raibh scót   ann,
   Neer awg shay korr-ig guh rev sgohth oun,

   Ná gur rith le   fórsa chun mé a mhilleadh,
   Naw gur ri lay fohr-sah kuhn may ah   vill-ah,

   Is ea ansin do chaith se an leim ba mho,
   Sun-shin dhuh koh shay on lame buh voh,

   Le fána mhór na Faille   Brice.
   Lay fawn-ah voor nah Foll-eh Brick-ah.

   Chorus

4. Bhi garda   mór i mBaile an Róistigh,
   Vee gawr-dha moor i moll-yon Rohsh-thig,

   Is bhailigh forsai chun sinn a chlipeadh,
   Iss voll-ig fohr-see kuhn shing ah   klip-ah,

   Do bhuail sé rop dá adhairc sa tóin air,
   Dhuh vool shay rup dhaw ire-k sah thohn err,

   Is da   bhriste nua do dhein sé giobal.
   Sdhaw vreesh-the noo dhuh yen shay gibb-el.

   Chorus

5. I nDaingean Ui Chúis le haghaidh an   tráthnóna,
   In-ang-in Ee Koosh leh hy-ghen thraw-nohn-ah,

   Bhi an sagart   paróiste amach nár gcoinnibh,
   Veen sog-orth par-ohsh-tay am-ock nawr gwinn-iv,

   Is é duirt gurbh é an diabhal ba dhóigh leis,
   Shay dhoort gur-av ay on deel boh goh lesh,

   A ghaibh an treo ar phocán   buile!
   Ah gov on throh err fuhk-awn bwill-ah!

   Chorus

Ever the Winds

The course of true love never runs smoothly.

Words and music by Tommy Makem

1. As I went a - walk - ing way down by the green wood,
2. I brought my love flow - ers all tied up with rib - bons;
3. My con - stant com - pan - ions are sad - ness and sor - row;

Down where the i - vy and lau - rel en - twine, I
Soon the sweet flow - ers were fad - ed and gone. Like the
Trou - ble has nev - er for - sak - en me yet. But wher -

heard a bird sing - ing his sad, plain-tive love - song; He mourned for his
flow - ers my true love's af - fec - tions have with - ered, Which leaves me a -
ev - er I go till my days are all num - bered, The love of my

Rocky Road to Dublin

The misfortunate farm laborer who traveled to Dublin and took the only way out—the emigrant ship—became somewhat of a stage Irishman by the time he reached expression in Liverpool. Still, this is a rollicking song and a challenge to breath and tongue.

Adapted by Pat Clancy, Tom Clancy,
Liam Clancy, and Tommy Makem

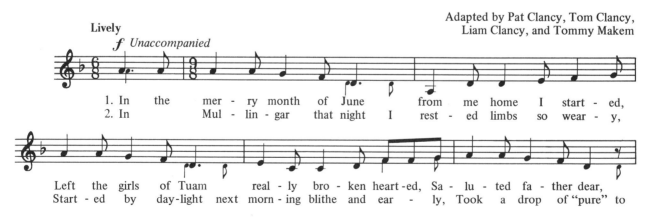

1. In the mer - ry month of June from me home I start - ed,
2. In Mul - lin - gar that night I rest - ed limbs so wear - y,

Left the girls of Tuam real - ly bro - ken heart -ed, Sa - lu - ted fa - ther dear,
Start - ed by day-light next morn - ing blithe and ear - ly, Took a drop of "pure" to

kissed me dar - ling moth - er, Drank a pint of beer, me grief and tears to smoth-er. Then
keep me heart from sink - ing; That's the Pad - dy's cure when - ev - er he's on for drink - ing.

off to reap the corn, leave where I was born, Cut a stout black thorn to
See the las - sies smile, laugh - ing all the while At me cu - rious style, 'twould

ban - ish ghosts and gob - lins; A brand new pair of brogues rat - tling o'er the bogs And
set your heart a - bub - bl - ing; Asked me was I hired, wa - ges I re - quired, Till

fright - 'ning all the dogs___ on the rock - y road to Dub - b' - lin.
I was near - ly tired___ of the rock - y road to Dub - b' - lin.

Chorus

One, two, three, four, five, Hunt the hare and turn her

Down the rock - y road and All the way to Dub - b' - lin, Whack fol - lol - de - rah.

3. In Dublin next arrived, I thought it such a pity
   To be so soon deprived a view of that fine city.
   So then I took a stroll, all among the quality;
   Me bundle it was stole, all in a neat locality.
   Something crossed me mind, when I looked behind,
   No bundle could I find upon me stick a-wobbling.
   Enquiring for the rogue, they said me Connaught brogue
   Wasn't much in vogue on the rocky road to Dublin.
   Chorus

4. From there I got away, me spirits never failing,
   Landed on the quay, just as the ship was sailing.
   The captain at me roared, said that no room had he;
   When I jumped aboard, a cabin found for Paddy.
   Down among the pigs, played funny rigs,
   Danced some hearty jigs, the water round me bubbling;
   When off Holyhead wished meself was dead
   Or better for instead on the rocky road to Dublin.
   Chorus

5. Well, the boys of Liverpool, when we safely landed,
   Called myself a fool, I could no longer stand it.
   Blood began to boil, temper I was losing;
   Poor old Erin's Isle they began abusing.
   "Hurrah, me soul," says I, my shillelagh I let fly.
   Some Galway boys were nigh and saw I was a hobble in,
   With a loud "hurray" joined in the affray.
   We quickly cleared the way for the rocky road to Dublin.
   Chorus

The Bard of Armagh

If Tommy Makem wanted a theme song, he would have it in "The Bard of
Armagh," since he is a bard from Armagh. It is the song of an old man look-
ing back on his youth and the fun he had at wakes and weddings. He reflects
that "merry-hearted boys make the best of old men."

Adapted by Pat Clancy, Liam Clancy,
Tom Clancy, and Tommy Makem

1. Oh,__ list to the lay of a poor I - rish harp - er And
2. At a fair or a wake I could twist my shil - le - lagh Or

scorn not the strains of his old with - ered hand, But__ re - mem - ber his fin - gers,__ they
trip through a jig with my brogues bound with straw, And__ all the pret - ty col - leens a -

once could move sharp - er To__ raise up the mem'ry__ of his dear na - tive land.
round me as - sem - bled Loved their bold Phel - im Bra - dy,__ the__ bard of Ar - magh.

3. Oh, how I long to muse on the days of my boyhood,
   Though four-score and three years have flitted since then;
   Yet they bring sweet reflections as every young joy should,
   For the merry-hearted boys make the best of old men.

4. And when Sergeant Death in his cold arms shall embrace me,
   Then lull me to sleep with sweet Erin go Bragh.
   By the side of my Kathleen, my young wife, oh, place me;
   Then forget Phelim Brady, the bard of Armagh.

Lament for Brendan Behan

This is a tribute to one of Ireland's great writers.

Words and music by Fred Geis

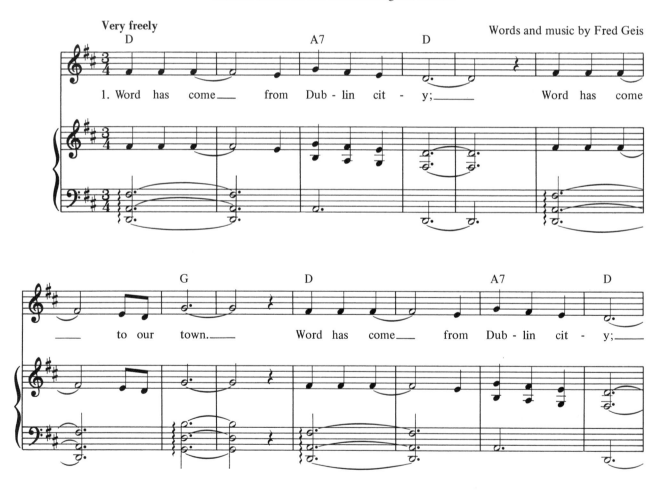

They tell me bold Bren-dan is dead.____ 2. Born in 'twen-ty-three in a slum in Dub-lin, With a ten-e-ment o-ver his head;____ Born with a spir-it his flesh could not con-tain,____ They tell me bold Bren-dan is dead.____ 3. He died at the "Meath" in

59

far off Dub - lin, In a cold white hos - pi - tal bed.____ In the

Geor - gian ten - e - ments the chil - dren hushed their sing - ing;____ They

know that bold Bren - dan is dead.____ 4. No stran - ger to life, he

lived right e - nough, No stran - ger to the glass in his hand;____ No

stran - ger to the cause he fought all his life, Yet they tell me bold Bren - dan is

dead.___ 5. Ire - land has lost her sweet an - gry sing - er; No

long - er his po - ems of fine de - sign___ Will sing out in Gae - lic or

sound thro' the lanes, For a - las! Bold__ Bren - dan is dead.___

Whiskey, You're the Devil

There's only one song in this book we Clancys can really claim we learned at mother's knee. Our mother's family owned a pub in Carrick-on-Suir which was the source of many a good song. She says that her mother used whiskey in a multitude of ways, such as rubbing it on the chest for a cough or giving it with hot water for a cold. The word "whiskey" actually comes from the Gaelic *uisge beatha,* which means "water of life."

Adapted with new words by Joan Clancy, Pat Clancy,
Tom Clancy, Liam Clancy, and Tommy Makem

Verse

1. Oh, now, brave boys, we're on the march And off to Por-tu-gal and Spain. The
2. The French are fight-ing bold - ly, Men dy-ing hot and cold - ly. Gives
3. Said the moth - er, "Do not wrong me; Don't take my daugh-ter from me. For

drums are beat-ing, ban-ners fly-ing; The dev-il a-home will come to-night.___
ev-'ry man his flask of pow-der, His far-lock on his shoul-der.___ Love, fare thee
if you do, I will tor-ment you, And af-ter death a ghost will haunt you."

well with me tith-er-y eye, the doo-de-lum, the da, Me tith-er-y eye, the doo-de-lum, the

da, Me rikes fall, tour a lad-die, Oh, there's whis-key in the jar. Hey!

D. C.

63

The Leaving of Liverpool

In the days of the clipper ships England was ruler of the seas and Liverpool was one of her largest ports. A collection of Liverpool sea songs and chanties would fill a volume in itself. This is perhaps one of the most haunting; the version we give here was rewritten to some extent by us. Bob Dylan used the tune and idea for one of his best songs, "Fare Thee Well, My Darling True."

Adapted with new words by Pat Clancy, Tom Clancy,
Liam Clancy, and Tommy Makem

turn some day.
float - ing hell.
you a - gain.

So— fare thee well, my—

own true love, And when I re - turn, u - nit - ed we will

be._____ It's not the leav - ing of Liv - er - pool that grieves—

me, But, my dar - ling, when I think of thee._____

Blow Ye Winds

This is a transportation song, probably having originated among prisoners being transported to Australia or Van Diemen's Land, where they were sent for having committed a variety of crimes—from stealing a loaf of bread to murder.

Words and music by Sarah Makem

Blow, ye winds, hi - ho, a - rov - ing I will go; I'll stay no more 'round Eng-land's shore, so let the mu - sic play. I'll be off on the morn - ing train, to cross the storm - y main; I'll be on the move to my own true love, three

Boulavogue

The rising of 1798 was really a number of isolated struggles. Only the Wexford rising had any great success, and part of this success was due to the courage of the "croppy priest," Father John Murphy. After the final defeat of the rebels at Vinegar Hill Father Murphy and other surviving leaders were hanged. The song was written by P. J. McCall and dates from the second half of the nineteenth century. The tune was known for generations as "Youghal Harbor." Boulavogue is the name of a small town in Wexford.

Adapted by Pat Clancy, Tom Clancy,
Liam Clancy, and Tommy Makem

1. At Boulavogue as the sun was setting__ On the bright May
   meadows__ of Shelmaliar,__ A rebel hand set the
   heather blazing__ And brought the neighbours__ from far and near. Then

2. He led us on 'gainst the coming soldiers; The cowardly
   yeomen__ we put to flight.__ 'Twas at the Harra the
   boys of Wexford__ Showed Bookies' reg'ment__ how men could fight. Look

3. At Vinegar Hill o'er the pleasant Slaney
   Our heroes vainly stood back to back,
   And the Yoes at Tullow took Father Murphy
   And burned his body upon the rack.
   God grant you glory, brave Father Murphy,
   And open heaven to all your men;
   For the cause that called you may call tomorrow
   In another fight for the green again.

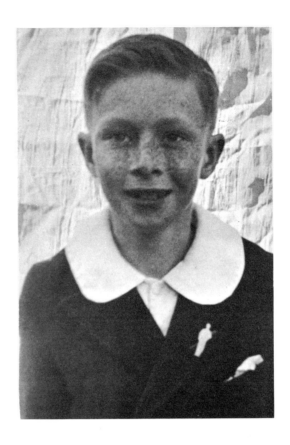

The Croppy Boy

There are versions of this song all over Ireland. The term "croppy" is said to
be a nickname given to the rebels of Wexford because of their close-cropped
hair, and for many generations the term was synonymous with "rebel." In
another version the croppy boy does not die at the end but goes into exile

Adapted by Pat Clancy, Tom Clancy,
Liam Clancy, and Tommy Makem

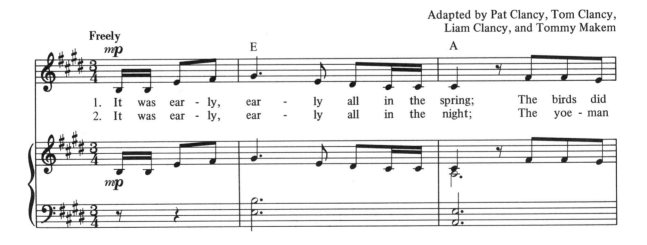

1. It was ear - ly, ear - ly all in the spring; The birds did
2. It was ear - ly, ear - ly all in the night; The yoe - man

whis-tle_____ and sweet-ly _ sing, Chang-ing their notes from_ tree to
cav-al-ry____ gave me a fright. The yoe-man cav-al-ry___ were_ my down-

tree, And the song they sang__ was old Ire - land free.
fall, And tak - en was I by__ Lord Corn - wall.

3. As I was walking up Wexford Hill
Oh, who would blame me to cry my fill?
I looked behind and I looked before,
But my aged mother I shall see no more.

4. As I was walking up Wexford Street,
My own first cousin I chanced to meet;
My own first cousin did me betray,
And for one bare guinea sold my life away.

5. As I was mounted on the platform high,
My aged father was standing by;
My aged father did me deny,
And the name he gave me was the croppy boy.

6. It was in Dungannon this young man died,
And in Dungannon his body lies;
So all good people who do pass by,
Just drop a tear for the croppy boy.

Mrs. Rockett's Pub

A tiny little gray-haired, good-natured woman, Mrs. Rockett still runs her pub a few miles from Tramore, the seaside resort in County Waterford. She still puts up the greatest feed of *crubeen* (pig's feet) and back bones in Ireland. Many's the great night Liam has spent in Mrs. Rockett's pub—and got fined one pound sterling one night for staying too long.

Words by Tommy Makem
Music traditional

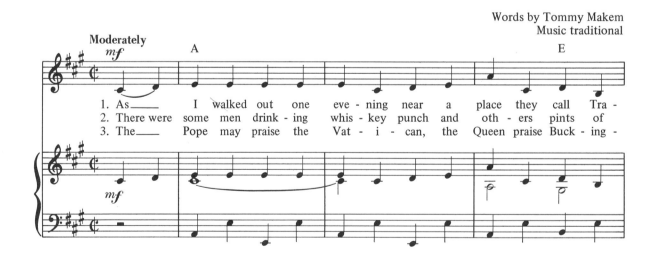

1. As____ I walked out one eve - ning near a place they call Tra -
2. There were some men drink - ing whis - key punch and oth - ers pints of
3. The____ Pope may praise the Vat - i - can, the Queen praise Buck - ing -

more, My legs were ver - y tired___ and my feet were ver - y
beer, And ___ some were drink - ing por - ter and they all were in good
ham; There's some may praise the Taj Ma - hal or a pal - ace in Si -

sore; I was feel - ing ver - y thirst - y af - ter eat - ing salt - y
cheer; And ___ la - dies sip - ping sher - ry wine, the fin - est ev - er
am. And ___ all the lords and la - dies, they may boast ___ a - bout their

grub, When ___ La - dy Luck di - rect - ed me to Mis - sus Rock - ett's pub.
seen, And an old lad in the cor - ner, he was eat - ing a cru - been.
club, But they need - n't think they've lived at all till they've been to Rock - ett's pub.

Chorus
Here's a health to Mis - sus Rock - ett, and it's long she may re - main To quench the thirst of

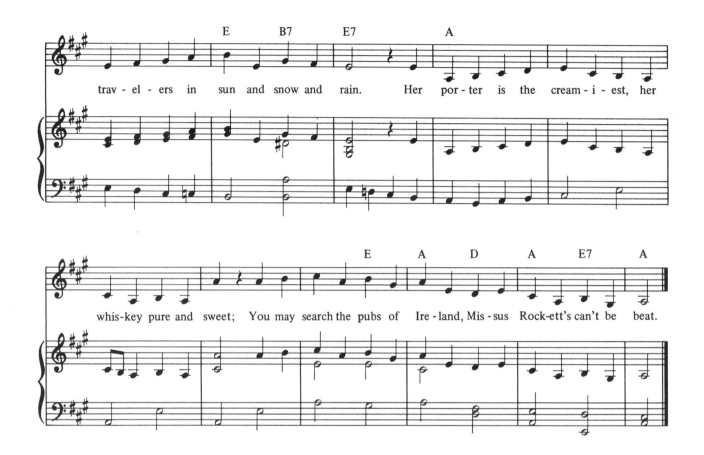

trav - el - ers in sun and snow and rain. Her por - ter is the cream - i - est, her

whis-key pure and sweet; You may search the pubs of Ire - land, Mis - sus Rock-ett's can't be beat.

A Man of Double Deed

Children love gruesome things. This is a typical song that children sing for
their own amusement.

Adapted by Joan Clancy, Pat Clancy, Tom Clancy,
Liam Clancy, and Tommy Makem

There was a man of dou - ble deed, who sowed his gar - den full of seed.

When the seed be - gan to grow, 'twas like a gar - den full of snow; When the snow be -

gan to fall, like birds it was up - on a wall; And when the birds be - gan to fly, 'twas

78

like a ship-wreck in the sky; And when the sky be-gan to crack, 'twas

like a stick up-on my back; And when my back be-gan to smart, 'twas like a pen-knife

in my heart; And when my heart be-gan to bleed, then I was dead, and dead in-deed.

poco rit.

slower

Paper of Pins

How much is love worth—or is it priceless?

Adapted by Peg Clancy and Robert Clancy

1. I'll give to you a pa-per of pins, If that's the way that love be-gins, If
2. I'll give to you a gold-en ball, To bounce from the kitch-en to the hall, If

you will mar-ry, mar-ry, mar-ry, mar-ry, If you'll mar-ry me.
you will mar-ry, mar-ry, mar-ry, mar-ry, If you'll mar-ry me.

(Girl)

1. I don't want your pa-per of pins, If that's the way that love be-gins, For
2. I don't want your gold-en ball, To bounce from the kitch-en to the hall, For

I won't mar - ry, mar - ry, mar - ry, mar - ry, I won't mar - ry you.
I won't mar - ry, mar - ry, mar - ry, mar - ry, I won't mar - ry you.

3. *Boy:*   I'll give to you a rockin' chair,
          To sit in the garden and take fresh air,
          If you will marry, marry, marry, marry,
          If you will marry me.

3. *Girl:*   I don't want a rockin' chair,
          To sit in the garden and take fresh air,
          For I won't marry, marry, marry, marry,
          I won't marry you.

4. *Boy:*   I'll give to you a silver spoon,
          To feed the baby in the afternoon,
          If you will marry, marry, marry, marry,
          If you will marry me.

4. *Girl:*   I don't want a silver spoon,
          To feed the baby in the afternoon,
          For I won't marry, marry, marry, marry,
          I won't marry you.

The Wren Song

The Wren Boys tradition still lives in certain parts of Ireland; in fact, each year, on St. Stephen's day, a festival is held at Listowel. The Wren Boys place an effigy of a wren in the middle of a holly bush, which they then decorate. Dressed in bizarre costumes, they go from door to door, asking for money, and singing one of the many versions of this song.

Adapted by Joan Clancy, Tom Clancy, Pat Clancy, Liam Clancy, and Tommy Makem

1. The wren, the wren, the king of all birds, St. Steph - en's Day was caught in the furze; Al - though he was lit - tle, his hon - or was great. Jump up, me lads, and give him a treat.

2. As I was gone to Kill - en - aule I met a wren up - on the wall; Up with me wat - tle and knocked him down. And brought him in - to Car - rick town.

3. Drool - in, drool - in, where's your nest? "'Tis in the bush that I love best; In the tree, the hol - ly tree, Where all the boys do fol - low me."

Up with the ket - tle and down with the pan And

give us a pen - ny to bur - y the wren.
4. We fol - lowed the wren three
5. We have a lit - tle box
6. Mis - sus Clan - cy's a

miles or more, Three miles or more, three miles or more,
un - der me hand, Un - der me hand, un - der me hand, We
ver - y good wom - an, A ver - y good wom - an, a ver - y good wom - an,

Fol - lowed the wren three miles or more At six o'clock in the morn - ing.
have a lit - tle box un - der me hand; A pen - ny a tup - pence will do it no harm.
Mis - sus Clan - cy's a ver - y good wom - an: She gave us a pen - ny to bur - y the wren.

Weela Wallia

The children in the tenements of Dublin are very wise. Since there is no place to hide anything from them, they know all the secrets of life before they are four years old. One might hear these children singing this charming song while sitting on the steps of the tenements.

Adapted by Pat Clancy, Tom Clancy, Liam Clancy, and Tommy Makem

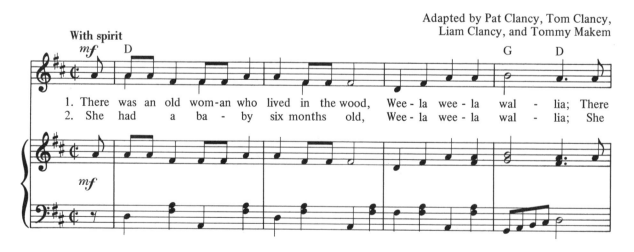

1. There was an old wom-an who lived in the wood, Wee - la wee - la wal - lia; There
2. She had a ba - by six months old, Wee - la wee - la wal - lia; She

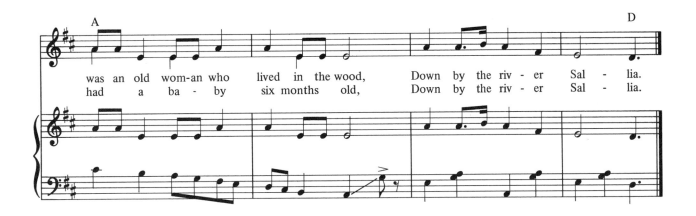

was an old wom-an who lived in the wood, Down by the riv - er Sal - lia.
had a ba - by six months old, Down by the riv - er Sal - lia.

3. She had a penknife three foot long,
   Weela weela wallia;
   She had a penknife three foot long
   Down by the river Sallia.

4. She stuck the knife in the baby's head,
   Weela weela wallia;
   The more she stabbed it the more it bled
   Down by the river Sallia.

5. Three big knocks came a-knocking at the door,
   Weela weela wallia;
   Two policemen and a man,
   Down by the river Sallia.

6. "Are you the woman what killed the child?"
   Weela weela wallia.
   "Are you the woman what killed the child
   Down by the river Sallia?"

7. "I am the woman what killed the child."
   Weela weela wallia.
   "I am the woman what killed the child
   Down by the river Sallia."

8. The rope got chucked and she got hung,
   Weela weela wallia;
   The rope got chucked and she got hung
   Down by the river Sallia.

9. The moral of this story is,
   Weela weela wallia,
   Don't stick knives in babies' heads
   Down by the river Sallia.

When I Was Young

This is a children's song that is not gory or gruesome at all.

Adapted by Joan Clancy, Pat Clancy,
Tom Clancy, and Tommy Makem
Additional words by Liam Clancy

1. When I was young, I had no sense; I bought a fid-dle for
2. My Aunt Jane she called me in; She gave me tea out of

eight-een pence. The on-ly tune that I could play Was "O-ver the Hills and
her wee tin, Half a bag of sug-ar on the top And three black lumps out of

Ver-y Far A-way." So ear-ly in the morn-ing, So ear-ly in the
her wee shop.

morn-ing, So ear - ly in the morn-ing, Be - fore the break of day.

Sally-O

This is a love song about a young man who needed only his sweetheart beside him to make life perfect.

Words and music by Tommy Makem

wind blow low; I'd__ feel no__ cold__ from the frost or snow If I

on - ly had my__ Sal - ly - O, Where the wild birds sing__ on the moun - tain.

3. Oh, I'd bring salmon from the stream,
   From the stream, from the stream,
   And berries fit for any queen,
   Where the wild birds sing on the mountain.
   Chorus

4. Oh, we'd have music all the day,
   All the day, all the day,
   And peace that drives all care away,
   Where the wild birds sing on the mountain.
   Chorus

The Curlew's Song

If you have ever stood in the middle of a bog and heard the curlew's cry,
you've known the meaning of loneliness.

Words and Music by Tommy Makem

1. I heard a cur-lew cry-ing long On a
2. Cold win-ter came and the moor-land froze;

moor where wild winds blew, And the sound of his sad, lone-some
winds howled loud and long. And of-ten ech-oed through the

3. Sweet sun-warmed summer came along
   From green-leafed days of spring;
   I soon forgot the lonesome song
   I heard the curlew sing.
   Ah, ah.

Blackwater Side

This is a conversation between two lovers overheard one morning on the bank of the River Blackwater in County Cork.

Lyrically, but with a feeling of one to the bar

Adapted by Liam Clancy

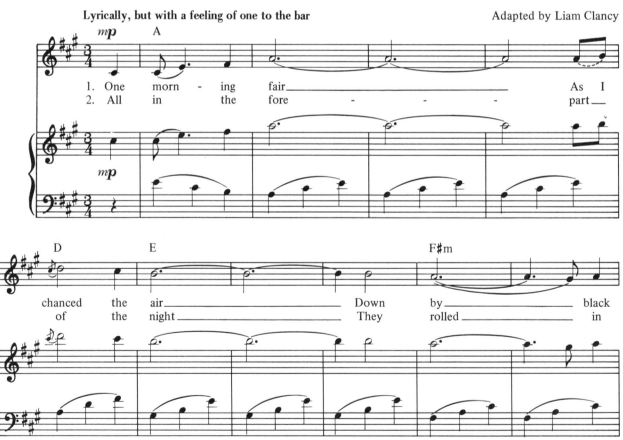

1. One morn - ing fair_____ As I
2. All in the fore - - - part_____

chanced the air_____ Down by_____ black
of the night_____ They rolled_____ in

3. "That's not the promise you made to me
   When you lay upon my breast;
   You could make me believe with your lying tongue
   That the sun rose in the west."

4. "Go home, go home to your father's garden,
   Go home and cry your fill;
   And think of the sad misfortune
   I brought on with my wanton will."

5. "There's not a flower in this whole world
   As easily led as I;
   And when fishes can fly and seas do run dry,
   It is then that you'll marry I."

The Month of January

This is the age-old story of a young girl spurned by her lover because she has his baby. Her parents then turn her out of their home.

Words and music by Sarah Makem

snow, / me,

1. It was in the month of Jan-u-ar-y, the hills were clad in
2. "Oh, cru-el was my fa-ther, who barred the door on

As o-ver hills and moun-tains my
And cru-el was my moth-er this

true love she did go. / dread-ful crime to see;

It was there I spied a pret-ty fair
Oh, cru-el was my own true

maid with a salt tear in__ her eye; She__
love to__ change his mind_ for gold, And__

had a ba - by in her arms_ and bit - ter she did cry.
cru - el was that win - ter's night_ that pierced my heart with cold."

3. Oh, the taller that the palm tree grows, the sweeter is the bark,
   And the fairer that a young man speaks, the falser is his heart;
   He will kiss you and embrace you 'til he thinks he has you won,
   Then he'll go away and leave you, all for some other one.

4. So come, all you pretty fair maids, a warning take by me,
   And never try to build your nests on top of a high tree;
   For the roots they will all wither and the branches all decay,
   And the beauties of a false young man must all soon fade away.

Bungle Rye

When a sailor who tries to buy a drink ends up with a baby in a basket and his money all gone, he must be a Jonah.

Adapted by Robert Clancy, Pat Clancy, Tom Clancy, Liam Clancy, and Tommy Makem

1. Now, Jack was a sail - or who roved on the town, And she was a
2. Thought Jack to him - self, "Now what can it be But the fin - est ould

dam - sel who skipped up and down. Said the dam - sel to Jack as
whis - key from far Ger - man - y, Smug - gled up in a bas - ket and

she passed him by, "Would you care for to pur - chase some quare Bun - gle
sold on the sly, And the name that it goes by is quare Bun - gle

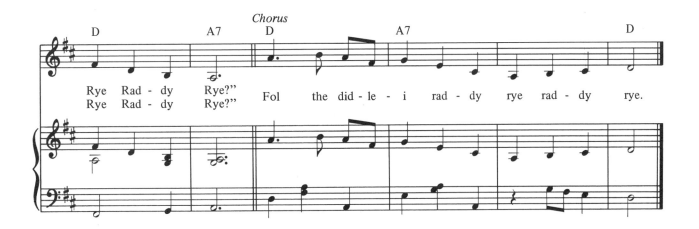

Chorus

Rye   Rad - dy   Rye?"   Fol   the   did - le - i   rad - dy   rye   rad - dy   rye.
Rye   Rad - dy   Rye?"

3. Jack gave her a pound and he thought nothing strange:
   She said, "Hold then the basket till I run for your change."
   Jack looked in the basket and a child he did spy.
   "Oh, bedamned then," said Jack, "this is quare Bungle Rye Raddy Rye."
   Chorus

4. Now, to get the child christened was Jack's next intent;
   For to get the child christened to the parson he went.
   Said the parson to Jack, "What will he go by?"
   "Oh, bedamned then," said Jack, "call him quare Bungle Rye Raddy Rye."
   Chorus

5. Said the parson to Jack, "That's a very quare name."
   "Oh, bedamned then," said Jack, "and the quare way he came,
   Smuggled up in a basket and sold on the sly,
   And the name that he'll go by is quare Bungle Rye Raddy Rye."
   Chorus

6. Now, all you bold sailors who rove on the town,
   Beware of the damsels who skip up and down.
   Take a peep in their baskets as they pass you by,
   Or else they may pawn on you quare Bungle Rye Raddy Rye.
   Chorus

Master McGrath

Master McGrath was a greyhound who became an Irish national hero by beating an English bitch named White Rose and carrying back the coveted Waterloo Cup to Ireland three times. There's a big stone monument to him in County Waterford. It's a hundred years since he chased the hare, and yet his picture is still proudly displayed in half the pubs and barbershops of Ireland.

Adapted by Pat Clancy, Tom Clancy,
Liam Clancy, and Tommy Makem

1. Eight - een six - ty - nine be - ing the date of the year, The Wa - ter - loo
2. And when they ar - rived there in big Lon - don town, The great Eng - lish

sports - men, they all did ap - pear | To win the great prize and to
sports - men, they all gath - ered 'round. | One of the gen - tle - men

bear it a - way, | Nev - er count - ing on | Ire - land and Mas - ter Mc - Grath.
gave a ha - ha, | "Is___ that the great | dog you call Mas - ter Mc - Grath?"

3. Lord Lurgon stepped forward and he said, "Gentlemen,
   If there are any among you have money to spend,
   For your great English greyhound I don't care a straw.
   Five thousand to one upon Master McGrath."

4. White Rose stood uncovered, the great English pride;
   Her trainer and owner were both by her side.
   They led her away and the crowd cried, "Hurrah!"
   For the pride of all England and Master McGrath.

5. As Rose and the Master, they both ran along,
   "I wonder," said Rose, "what took you from your home.
   You should have stayed there in your Irish domain
   And not come to gain laurels on Albion's plains."

6. "I know," said McGrath, "we have wild heather bogs,
   But you'll find in old Ireland we have good men and dogs.
   Lead on, bold Britannia, give none of your jaw;
   Snuff that up your nostrils," said Master McGrath.

7. The hare she led on, what a beautiful view,
   As swift as the wind o'er the green fields she flew.
   He jumped on her back and he held up his paw;
   "Three cheers for old Ireland," said Master McGrath.

8. I've known many greyhounds that filled me with pride
   In the days that are gone and it can't be denied,
   But the greatest and the bravest the world ever saw
   Was our champion of champions, brave Master McGrath.

The Lowlands of Holland

The English were at war with Holland in the middle of the seventeenth century. This song comes from young men being pressed into service in that war.

Adapted by Pat Clancy, Tom Clancy, Liam Clancy, and Tommy Makem

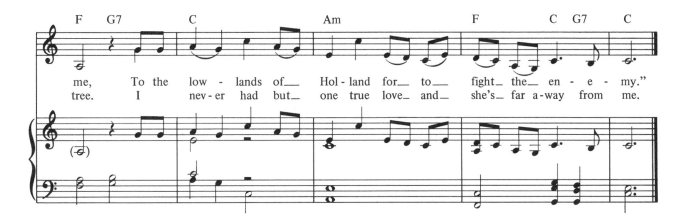

me,   To the   low - lands of___   Hol - land for___ to___   fight__ the__ en - e - my."
tree.   I   nev - er had but__   one true love_ and__   she's__ far a - way   from   me.

3. Says the mother to the daughter, "Leave off your sore lament;
There's men enough in Galway to be your heart's content."
"There's men enough in Galway, but alas, there's none for me,
Since the high winds and the stormy seas have parted my love and me."

4. "I'll wear no stays around my waist, no combs all in my hair,
No handkerchief around my neck to shade my beauty fair;
And neither will I marry until the day I die,
Since the high winds and the stormy seas have parted my love and I."

The Rapparee

The Rapparee were political outlaws well-loved by the people because of their Robin Hood qualities.

Words and music by Seamus McGrath, Tom Brett,
Michael O'Brian, and James English

1. My spurs are rust-ed, my coat is rent, my plume is damp with rain;
2. The moun-tain cav-ern is my home, high up in the crys-tal air,
3. Hunt-ed from out our fa-ther's home, pur-sued by steel and shot,

And the this-tle-down and the bar-ley-beard are thick on my horse-'s mane.
And my bed of lime-stone i-ron-ribbed and the brown heath smell-ing fair.
A blood-y war-fare we must wage, or the gib-bet be our lot.

But my ri-fle's as bright as my
Let George or Will-iam
Hur-rah! this war is

sweet - heart's eyes; my arm is strong and free. What
on - ly send his troops to burn or loot; We'll
wel - come work, the hunt - ed out - law knows; He

care have I for your king or laws? I'm an out - lawed rap - pa - ree.
meet them up on e - qual ground and we'll fight them foot to foot.
steps un - to his coun - try's love o'er the corps - es of his foes.

Chorus

Lift your glass - es, friends, with mine, And give your hand to me. I'm

Eng - land's foe, I'm Ire - land's friend, I'm an out - lawed rap - pa - ree.

107

The Lough Neagh Fishers

For generations the local people at Lough Neagh have fished eels for their living. Recently a syndicate obtained a license from the government for the exclusive eel fishing rights. The local fishermen still fish, as they have no other way to live, but now they are called poachers.

Words and music by James Corr

fol - lowed the eel here since time be - gan, I've hunt - ed the
man has a right and a du - ty as well to pro - vide for his

length of our shore;＿＿＿ And now a com - pan - y from
fam - 'ly at home,＿＿＿ And the on - ly way we know

Eng - land has come, bought our rights to hunt the Lough shore.＿＿＿
how to pro - vide is the eel down a - long the Lough shore.＿＿＿

Chorus C
Our moth - ers, our wives, and our sweet - hearts as well, They told＿ their men what to

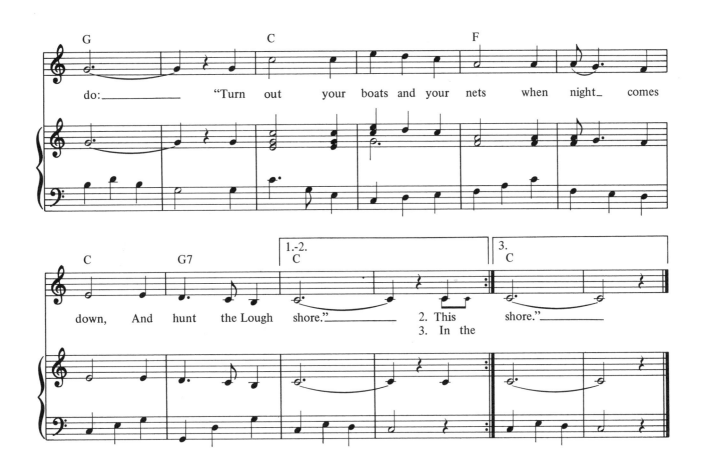

do:_____ "Turn out your boats and your nets when night_ comes

down, And hunt the Lough shore."_____

1.-2.
C
2. This
3. In the

3.
C
shore."_____

3. In the town of Dungannon and in the high court they say that poachers are we,
   But what would they say and what would they do if the tables turned might be?
   For a man has a right and a duty as well to provide for his family at home,
   And the only way we know how to provide is the eel down along the Lough shore.
   Chorus

Maid of Fife-E-O

Usually in a love song about a soldier and a young girl it is the girl who comes off the worst. In this song the soldier dies.

Adapted by Pat Clancy, Tom Clancy,
Liam Clancy, and Tommy Makem

1. There once was a troop of
come down the stairs, pret-ty

I - rish dra-goons Came march - ing____ down through Fife - e - O; And the
Peg - gy, my dear; Oh, come down the stairs, pret-ty Peg - gy - O. Oh,____

cap-tain fell in love with a ver - y bon-ny lass, And her name it was
come____ down the stairs, comb back your yel-low hair, Bid a long fare -

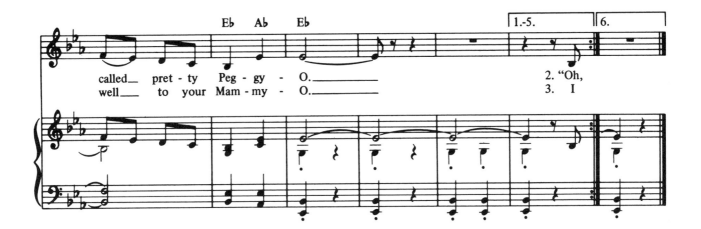

called___ pret - ty Peg - gy - O._____

well___ to your Mam - my - O._____

2. "Oh,

3. I

3. "I never did intend a soldier's lady for to be;
   I never will marry a soldier-O.
   I never did intend to go to a foreign land,
   And I never will marry a soldier-O."

4. The colonel he cried, "Mount, mount, boys, mount."
   The captain he cried, "Tarry-O.
   Oh, tarry for a while, for another day or two,
   Till I see if this bonny lass will marry-O."

5. Long 'ere we came to the town of Ackerglass
   We had our captain to carry-O,
   And long 'ere we reached the streets of Aberdeen
   We had our captain to bury-O.

6. Green grow the birks on bonny Ethen-side,
   And low lie the lowlands of Fife-e-O.
   Well, the captain's name was Ned, and he died for a maid;
   He died for the chambermaid of Fife-e-O.

The Earl of Moray

In December, 1591, King James VI of Scotland commissioned the Earl of Huntley to capture the Earl of Bothwell, who had made an abortive attempt on the king's life. On the night of February 7, 1592, under protection of the commission, Huntley attacked the house of the Earl of Moray, a relative of Bothwell. There was an existing feud between the two, and Huntley burned the house to the ground and killed Moray.

Adapted by Pat Clancy, Tom Clancy,
Liam Clancy, and Tommy Makem

1. Ye high-lands and ye low-lands,___ and where have ye been, They have
2. Oh, woe be-tide ye Hunt-ley,___ and where-fore did ye say, "I___
3. Ye high-lands and ye low-lands,___ and where have ye been, They have

slain the Earl of Mor-ay and laid him on the green.___ He
bade ye bring him to me, but for-bade ye him to slay"?___ He
slain the Earl of Mor-ay and laid him on the green.___ He

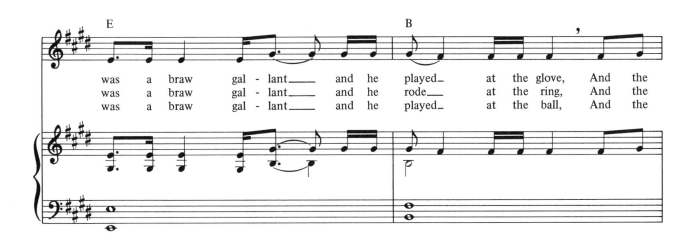

was a braw gal - lant____ and he played__ at the glove, And the
was a braw gal - lant____ and he rode__ at the ring, And the
was a braw gal - lant____ and he played__ at the ball, And the

Chorus

bon - ny Earl of Mor-ay,__ he was the Queen's own love.
bon - ny Earl of Mor-ay,__ he might have been a king. Long will his la - dy__ look__
bon - ny Earl of Mor-ay__ was a flow'r a - mong them all.

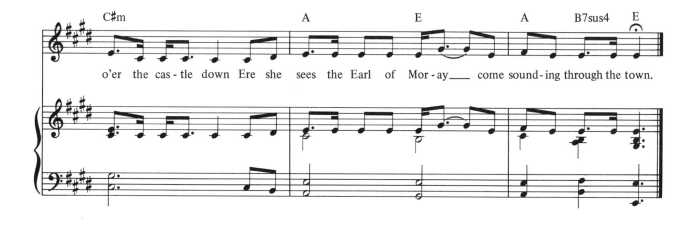

o'er the cas - tle down Ere she sees the Earl of Mor-ay__ come sound-ing through the town.

The Cobbler

This is the song of a man who found a solution to his wife problem.

Adapted with new words by Tommy Makem

1. Oh, me name is Dick Dar - by, I'm a cob - bler; I
2. Now, my fa - ther was hung for sheep steal - ing, My

ser - ved me time at old camp. Some call me an old ag - i - ta - tor, But
moth - er was burned for a witch, My sis - ter's a dan - dy house-keep - er, And

now I'm re - solved to re - pent.
I'm a mech - an - i - cal switch.

Chorus

With me ing - twing of an ing - thing of an

i - day,   With me   ing - twing of an ing - thing of an   i - day,   With me

roo - boo - boo roo - boo - boo ran - dy,   And me   lab stone keeps beat - ing   a - way._____

3. Ah, it's forty long years I have travelled,
All by the contents of me pack;
Me hammers, me awls and me pinchers,
I carry them all on me back.
Chorus

4. Oh, my wife she is humpy, she's lumpy,
My wife she's the devil, she's black;
And no matter what I may do with her,
Her tongue it goes clickety-clack.
Chorus

5. It was early one fine summer's morning,
A little before it was day;
I dipped her three times in the river
And carelessly bade her "Good day!"
Chorus

Lord Nelson

In March, 1966, the statue of Lord Nelson was unofficially removed from Dublin's O'Connell Street. At the other end of O'Connell still stands the statue of Daniel O'Connell, who was called the great liberator.

With spirit

Words and music by Tommy Makem

1. Lord Nel - son stood in pom - pous state up - on his pil - lar high, And down a - long O' - Con - nell Street he cast a wick - ed eye. He thought how this bar - bar - ic race had fought the Brit - ish
2. For man - y years Lord Nel - son stood, And no one seemed to care; He'd squint at Dan O' - Con - nell, who was sit - ting right down there. He thought, "The I - rish like me, or they would - n't let me

Crown, Yet they were con-tent to let him stay right here in Dub-lin town.

stay, That is, ex-cept those blight-ers that they call the I. R. A."

Chorus

So re-mem-ber brave Lord Nel-son, boys, he had nev-er known de-feat; And for

his re-ward they stuck him up in the mid-dle of O'-Con-nell Street.

3. And then in nineteen sixty-six, on March the seventh day,
   A bloody-great explosion made Lord Nelson rock and sway.
   He crashed, and Dan O'Connell cried in woeful misery,
   "There are twice as many pigeons now will come and sit on me!"

Chorus
So remember brave Lord Nelson, boys, he had never known defeat;
And for his reward they blew him up in the middle of O'Connell Street.

The Butcher Boy

This tragic and beautiful ballad is a variant of the widely known "Gosport Tragedy." It has become very popular throughout Ireland, where everyone seems to have a soft spot for a nice sad love song.

Adapted by Sarah Makem

1. In Lon-don cit - y, where I did dwell, A butch-er boy I loved right well; He court-ed me my life a-way, But now with me he will not stay.

2. I wish, I wish, I wish in vain, I wish I was a maid a-gain; A maid a-gain I ne'er will be 'Till cher-ries grow on an i-vy tree.

3. "I wish my baby it was born
   And smiling on its daddy's knee;
   And me, poor girl, to be dead and gone,
   With the long green grass growing over me."

4. She went upstairs to go to bed,
   And calling to her mother, said,
   "Give me a chair till I sit down
   And a pen and ink till I write down."

5. At every word she dropped a tear,
   At every line cried, "Willie, dear,
   Oh, what a foolish girl was I,
   To be led astray by a butcher boy."

6. He went upstairs and the door he broke;
   He found her hanging from a rope.
   He took his knife and he cut her down,
   And in her pocket these words he found:

7. "Oh, make my grave large, wide and deep.
   Put a marble stone at my head and feet;
   And in the middle, a turtledove,
   That the world may know that I died for love."

Winds of Morning

This was written by Tommy Makem on the New York subway, which always
inspires him to make songs about mountains and sea and sweet, clean air.

Words and music by Tommy Makem

3. By foreign shores my feet have wandered,
   Heard a stranger call me friend;
   Every time my mind was troubled,
   Found a smile around the bend.
   Chorus

4. There's a ship stands in the harbour,
   All prepared to cross the foam;
   Far off hills were fair and friendly,
   Still there's fairer hills at home.
   Chorus

The Rocks of Bawn

There are many versions of this well-known Irish traditional song. The title means "White Rocks."

Adapted by Pat Clancy, Tom Clancy,
Liam Clancy, and Tommy Makem

1. Come, all you loy-al he-roes, wher-ev-er that you be, And don't hire with an-y mas-ter 'til you know what your work will be. For you must rise up ear-ly

2. And it's rise up, love-ly Sween-ey, and give your horse some hay, And give him a good feed of oats be-fore you ride a-way. Don't feed him on soft tur-nips,

from the clear day-light_____ of dawn,_____ And I know_ that you'll
put him out on your_____ green lawn,_____ And I know_ that he'll

nev - er be a - ble_____ to plow the rocks of Bawn._____
nev - er be a - ble_____ to plow the rocks of Bawn._____

3. My curse attend you, Sweeney,
     for you have me nearly robbed,
   A-sittin' by the fireside
     with your doudeen in your gob,
   A-sittin' by the fireside
     from the clear daylight till dawn;
   And I know that you'll never be able
     to plough the rocks of Bawn.

4. My shoes thay are well worn out,
     my stockings they are thin,
   And my heart is always trembling
     for fear that they'll let in.
   And my heart is always trembling
     from the clear daylight of dawn,
   Afraid I'll never be able
     to plough the rocks of Bawn.

5. I wish the Queen of England
     would write to me in time
   And place me in some regiment,
     in all my youth and prime.
   I'd fight for Ireland's glory
     from the clear daylight of dawn,
   And I never would return again
     to plough the rocks of Bawn.

Maderine Rue

(MAUDE-UH-REEN-UH ROO)

Translated, this means "Little Red Fox." In this song England is the fox who devours the goose—Ireland.

Adapted with new words by Peg Clancy
and Robert Clancy

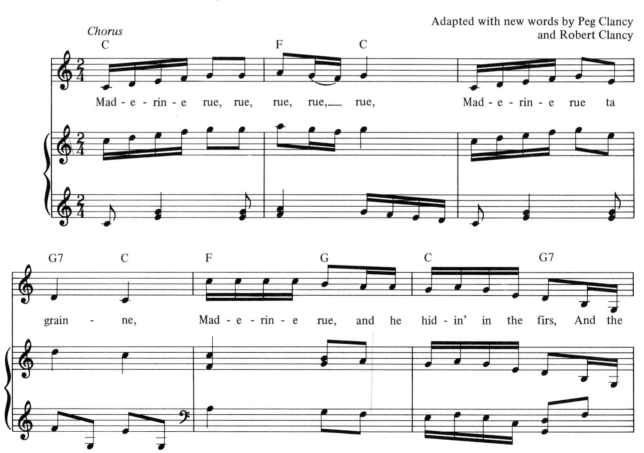

Chorus

Mad - e - rin - e rue, rue, rue, rue,___ rue, Mad - e - rin - e rue ta grain - ne, Mad - e - rin - e rue, and he hid - in' in the firs, And the

3. "Oh, no, indeed, bold fox," I said,
   "How dare you boldly taunt me?
   For I vow and swear that you'll dearly pay
   For that fine fat goose you're atin'."
   Chorus

4. "Bad cess to you, you bold, bad fox,
   That stole my geese and ate them,
   My great big cock, my fine fat hens,
   And the nicest little ducks in Erin."
   Chorus

5. Tally ho le na baun, tally ho le na baun,
   Tally ho le na baun, and we'll catch him,
   Tally ho le na baun, tally ho le na baun,
   And the tops of his two ears were peepin'.
   Chorus

McPherson's Lament

McPherson is one of Liam's heroes. A man who can get an exultant sense of victory and defiance in the face of defeat, and even death, is indeed a man to be admired.

Adapted by Pat Clancy, Tom Clancy, Liam Clancy, and Tommy Makem

1. "Fare - well, ye dun - geons dark and strong, Fare - well, fare - well to thee;
2. "Take off these bands from off my hands And give to me my sword,

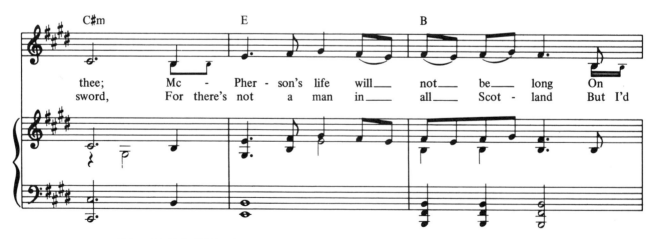

thee; Mc - Pher - son's life will not be long On
sword, For there's not a man in all Scot - land But I'd

3. "There's some come here for to see me hung,
   And some to buy my fiddle;
   But before that I do part with her,
   I'll break her through the middle."
   Chorus

4. He took his fiddle in both his hands,
   And he broke it o'er a stove,
   Saying, "There's nay ither hand shall play on thee
   When I am dead and gone."
   Chorus

5. The reprieve was coming o'er the Brig of Banff
   For to set McPherson free;
   But they put the clock a quarter before,
   And they hanged him from a tree.
   Chorus

Four Green Fields

The idea of using a secret name for Ireland goes back hundreds of years. The song expresses a deep love of country—the old woman being Ireland, and her four green fields the provinces of Ulster, Leinster, Munster, and Connaught.

Words and music by Tommy Makem

Bold Tenant Farmer

Before land reformation in Ireland most farmers only rented their small holdings from absentee British landlords. They lived in constant fear of eviction, since it was often impossible to pay exorbitant rents from the proceeds of a few miserable acres. The bailiff and rent collector became figures of terror to the small tenant farmer, and anyone who had the courage to speak up to them became a hero—or a heroine, as in this case.

Adapted by Robert Clancy

1. One eve - ning of late out of Ban - don I strayed, And bound for Clan - a - kil - ty I'm mak - ing my way; At Ba - lin - a - scath - y some

2. I scarce - ly had trav - elled a mile of the road When I heard a dis - pute in a farm - er's a - bode: The son of the land - lord, an

time I de-layed, For to wet me ould whis-tle with por-ter. Hey!
ill - look-ing toad, And the wife of the bold ten-ant farm-er. Hey!

Chorus

Tid-dle-le - oh - to, tid-dle-le-oh-to, tid-dle-le-oh-to-to-tum, Tid-dle-le -

oh-to, tid-le-le-oh-to, tid-dle-le-oh-to-to-tum, Tid-dle-le -

oh-tah-den, tid-dle-le-oh-to, Tid-dle-le-oh-to-tum, Tid-dle-le-oh-dah-den doo-dle-le-do.

3. "A robber," the bold tenant's wife she replied,
    "You're as bad as your daddy on the other side;
    But the National Land League will put down your pride,
    For they're able to bear every storm."
    Chorus

4. Well, I spit in my fist and I picked up my stick,
    And up the coach road like a deer I did trip;
    I cared not for bailiffs, landlord or ould Nick,
    And I sang like a lark in the morning.
    Chorus

CHARLES STUART PARNELL, M.P., PRESIDENT of the IRISH LAND LEAGUE, ADDRESSING A MEETING.

Freedom's Sons

This was written for the fiftieth anniversary of the 1916 rebellion.

Words and music by Tommy Makem

1. At Eas - ter time nine - teen - six - teen, When flow - ers
2. In Dub - lin town they fought and died With Pearse, Mc -

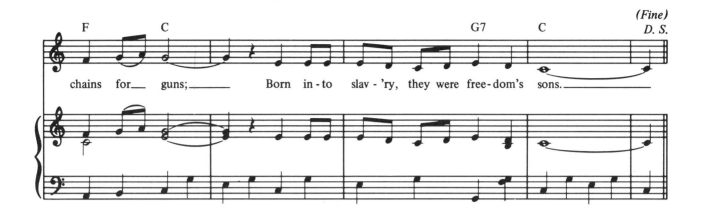

chains for__ guns;_____ Born in-to slav-'ry, they were free-dom's sons._____

3. A poet's dream had sparked the flame;
   A raging fire it soon became.
   And from that fire of destiny
   There rose a nation, proud and free.
   Chorus

4. Six counties are in bondage still;
   They died brave men, was this their will?
   Until they're free and oppressions cease,
   Only then brave men can rest in peace.
   Chorus

The Wind That Shakes the Barley

This is an excellent example of many songs that serve both as love lyric and rebel song. The scene described refers to the 1798 rising. The words are the work of Robert Dwyer Joyce, a professor of English Literature at Catholic University in Dublin. In danger of arrest for rebel activities, Joyce fled to the United States. He later returned to Ireland and died in Dublin in 1883.

Adapted by Tom Clancy, Pat Clancy,
Liam Clancy, and Tommy Makem

1. I sat with-in the val - ley green; I sat me with__ my true love.__ My sad heart strove the two be - tween, the old love and__ the new love:__ The old for her, the new that made me think on Ire - land

2. 'Twas hard the woe - ful words to frame to break the ties__ that bound us,__ But hard - er still to bear the shame of for - eign chains a - round us.__ And so I said, "The moun - tain glen I'll seek at morn - ing

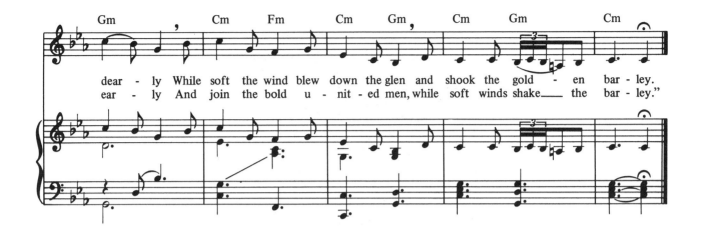

dear - ly While soft the wind blew down the glen and shook the gold - en bar - ley.
ear - ly And join the bold u - nit - ed men, while soft winds shake___ the bar - ley."

3. While sad I kissed away her tears, my fond arms round her flinging,
The foeman's shot burst on our ears from out the wildwood ringing.
A bullet pierced my true love's side in life's young spring so early,
And on my breast in blood she died while soft winds shook the barley.

4. But blood for blood without remorse I've taken at Oulart Hollow,
And laid my true love's clay cold corpse where I full soon may follow,
As round her grave I wander drear, noon, night and morning early,
With breaking heart when'er I hear the wind that shakes the barley.

Convict of Clonmel

This is a translation by J. J. Callanan from the eighteenth-century Irish poem
"Priosun Cluain Meala," whose author and subject are anonymous.

Adapted by Liam Clancy

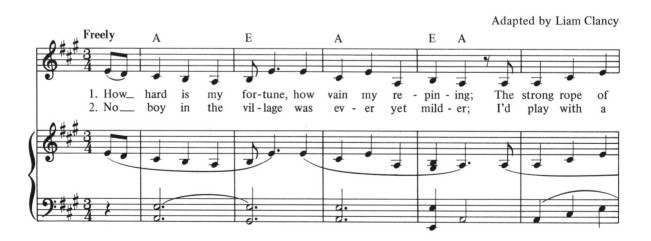

1. How_ hard is my for-tune, how vain my re - pin - ing; The strong rope of
2. No_ boy in the vil -lage was ev - er yet mild - er; I'd play with a

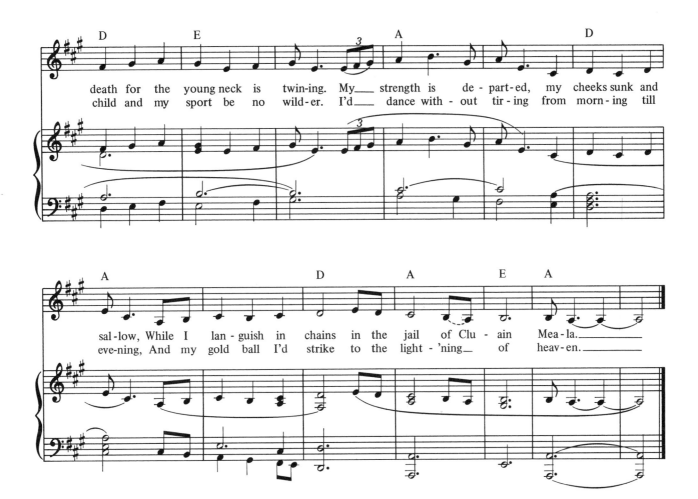

death for the young neck is twin-ing. My___ strength is de - part-ed, my cheeks sunk and
child and my sport be no wild-er. I'd___ dance with - out tir - ing from morn - ing till

sal -low, While I lan - guish in chains in the jail of Clu - ain Mea - la.___
eve-ning, And my gold ball I'd strike to the light - 'ning___ of heav - en.___

3. At my bed foot decaying my hurley is lying,
   Through the lads of the village my gold ball is flying,
   My horse 'mong the neighbors neglected may follow,
   While I pine in my chains in the jail of Cluain Meala.

4. Next Sunday the pattern at home will be keeping,
   All the young active hurlers the field will be sweeping,
   The dance of fair maidens the evening will hallow,
   While this heart once so gay will be cold in Cluain Meala.

O'Donnell Abú

The O'Donnells were clan chiefs in Tirconnel, which once covered what is now County Donegal. The song's references to sixteenth-century heroes made it especially applicable as a rallying cry for many occasions and periods. The words are the work of Michael Joseph McCann, a professor at St. Jarleth College, Tuam, County Mayo, and first appeared under the title "The Clan Connell War Song" in "The Nation" in 1843. It is sung to music written by a military bandmaster from Carrick-on-Suir, County Tipperary. When the first Irish Government was voting on a national anthem, "O'Donnell Abú" ran a close second to "The Soldiers' Song." "Abú" means "onward" in Gaelic.

Adapted by Pat Clancy, Tom Clancy,
Liam Clancy, and Tommy Makem

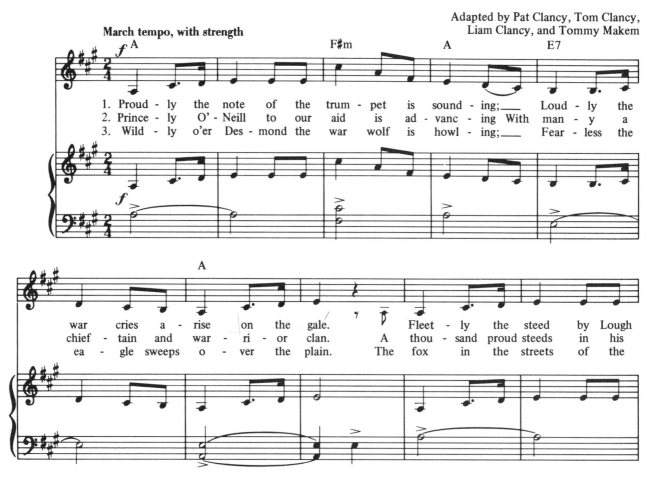

1. Proud - ly the note of the trum - pet is sound - ing;___ Loud - ly the
2. Prince - ly O' - Neill to our aid is ad - vanc - ing With man - y a
3. Wild - ly o'er Des - mond the war wolf is howl - ing;___ Fear - less the

war cries a - rise on the gale. Fleet - ly the steed by Lough
chief - tain and war - ri - or clan. A thou - sand proud steeds in his
ea - gle sweeps o - ver the plain. The fox in the streets of the

Swil - ly is bound - ing To join the thick squad-rons on__ Saim - er's green
van - guard are pranc - ing 'Neath the bor - der - ers brave__ from the banks of the
cit - y is prowl - ing, And all who would scare them are__ ban - ished or

vale. On, ev - 'ry moun - tain - eer, stran - gers to flight or fear;
Bann. Man - y a heart shall quail un - der its coat of mail,
slain. On with O' - Don - nell, then, fight the old fight a - gain;

Rush to the stand - ard of daunt - less Red Hugh. Bon - naught and Gal - low - glass,
Deep - ly the mer - ci - less foe - man shall rue, When on his ear shall ring,
Sons of Tir Con - nell, are val - iant and true. Make the proud Sax - on feel

throng from each moun - tain pass;__ On - ward for Er - in, O' - Don - nell A - bú!
borne on the breeze -'s wing, Tir Con nell's dread war - cry, "O' - Don - nell A - bú!"
Er - in's a - veng - ing steel;__ Strike for your coun - try, O' - Don - nell A - bú!

The 23rd of June

The 23rd of June was the weavers' national holiday, hence its association
with a "jug of punch."

Adapted by Sean O'Boyle, Pat Clancy, Tom Clancy,
Liam Clancy, and Tommy Makem

144

was "The Jug of Punch." Lad-ly - fol - da-dee, Lad-ly - fol - da-did-dle - ee - I - da-lid-dle-dum,
a___ ti - dy wench?

Skid-der - y - I - da - lid - dle-dum, skid-der - y - I - da - lid - dle - id - dle - um - dum - dee.

3. Oh, what more hardship can a boy endure
Than to sit him down, oh, behind the door?
Oh, what more hardship can a boy endure
Than to sit him down, oh, behind the door
And in his hand no jug of punch,
Aye, and on his knee no tidy wench?
Chorus

4. When I am dead, all my drinking's over;
I'll take one drink and I'll drink no more.
When I am dead, all my drinking's over;
I'll take one drink while it's to the fore.
In case I mightn't get it on that day,
I will take it now and I'll drink away.
Chorus

5. When I am dead, aye, and in my mould,
At my head and feet leave a flowing bowl.
When I am dead, aye, and in my mould,
At my head and feet leave a flowing bowl.
And every young man that passes by,
He can take a drink and remember I.
Chorus

Nancy
Whiskey

A friend of ours who has known this song and heard it for years thought until recently that Nancy Whiskey was a woman. When you sing it, just keep in mind that it is the juice of the barley which the poor fellow is in love with.

Adapted by Tom Clancy, Pat Clancy,
Liam Clancy, and Tommy Makem

Easy rolling tempo

1. I'm a weav - er, a
   I went down through

Cal - ton__ weav - er;   I'm a rash and a rov - ing blade.   I've got sil - ver
Glas - gow__ Cit - y   Nan - cy Whis-key I chanced to smell.   I went in, sat

in my— pock-ets, And I fol-low the rov-ing— trade.— Whis - key, Whis-key,

down be - side her; Sev - en long years I loved her— well.—

Nan - cy— Whis-key, Whis - key, Whis - key, Nan - cy - O. 2. As O.

3. The more I kissed her, the more I loved her;
   The more I kissed her, the more she smiled.
   Soon I forgot my mother's teaching;
   Nancy soon had me beguiled.
   Chorus

4. Now, I rose early in the morning
   To slake my thirst, it was my need.
   I tried to rise but I was not able;
   Nancy had me by the knees.
   Chorus

5. So I'm going back to the Calton weaving;
   I'll surely make them shuttles fly.
   For I'll make more at the Calton weaving
   Than ever I did in a roving way.
   Chorus

6. So come, all you weavers, you Calton weavers;
   Come, all you weavers, where e'er you be.
   Beware of Whiskey, Nancy Whiskey;
   She'll ruin you like she ruined me.
   Chorus

The Old Orange Flute

This is a great song that can make fun of both sides of a controversial
situation and be enjoyed equally by both sides.

Adapted by Tommy Makem

twelfth of Ju - ly as it year - ly did come Bob played with his flute to the
boys of the place made some com - ment up - on it, And Bob had to fly to the

sound of a drum. You may talk of your harp, your pi - a - no or lute, But there's
prov - ince of Con-naught. He fled with his wife and his fix - ings to boot, And a

none can com - pare with the old or - ange flute. 2. Now,
long with the lat - ter his old or - ange flute. 3. At the

Prot - es - tant Boys." Too - ra

lu,_____ too - ra - lay,_____ Oh, it's six miles from Ban - gor to Don - na - ha - dee.

3. At the chapel on Sunday to atone for past deeds
   Said Paters and Aves and counted his beads,
   Till after some time at the priest's own desire
   He went with the old flute to play in the choir.
   He went with the old flute for to play for the Mass,
   But the instrument shivered and sighed, oh, alas.
   And try though he would, though it made a great noise,
   The flute would play only "The Protestant Boys."

4. Bob jumped and he started and got in a flutter
   And threw the old flute in the blessed holy water.
   He thought that this charm would bring some other sound;
   When he tried it again, it played "Croppies Lie Down."
   Now, for all he could whistle and finger and blow,
   To play Papish music he found it no go.
   "Kick the Pope" and "Boil Water" it freely would sound,
   But one Papish squeak in it couldn't be found.

5. At the council of priests that was held the next day
   They decided to banish the old flute away.
   They couldn't knock heresy out of its head,
   So they bought Bob a new one to play in its stead.
   Now, the old flute was doomed, and its fate was pathetic;
   'Twas fastened and burned at the stake as heretic.
   As the flames soared around it they heard a strange noise;
   'Twas the old flute still whistling "The Protestant Boys."
   Toora lu, toora lay,
   Oh, it's six miles from Bangor to Donnahadee.

The Cockies of Bungaree

Since Paddy became a farmer, he's drawn to songs about the "hard life." The "cockies," or "cockatoo" farmers of Australia, are the poorest of poor. They are so called because their main crop—an involuntary one—is the cockatoo... and you can't even eat the damn things. Even worse off than the "cockies" is the traveling laborer who has to work for them.

Adapted by Pat Clancy, Tom Clancy,
Liam Clancy, and Tommy Makem

1. Come,
all you wea - ry trav - el - lers who's out of work, just mind;_____ If you
how I came this wea - ry way I means to let you know;_____ Be - ing

take a trip to Bun - gar - ee, it's plen - ty there you'll find._____ Take a
out of em - ploy - ment, I did - n't know where to go. _____ I

trial with the cock-ies, you can take it straight from me: You'll
went to the reg-is-ter of-fice, and there I did a-gree To

ver-y sure-ly rue the day you go to Bun-gar-ee._____ 2. Well,
take a job a-clear-ing for a cock-y in Bun-gar-ee._____ 3. His

one._____ 8. And now my job is o-ver and I'm at lib-er-

ty,_____ I'll nev-er for-get the day I met the cock-y from Bun-gar-ee.

3. His homestead was of surface mud, and his roof of mouldy thatch;
   The doors and windows hung by a nail with never a bolt or a catch.
   The chickens ran over the table, such a sight you never did see;
   One laid an egg in the old tin plate of the cocky from Bungaree.

4. And on the very first morning it was the usual go;
   He battled a plate for breakfast before the cocks did crow.
   The stars were shining gloriously, the moon was high, you see;
   I thought before the sun would rise, I'd die in Bungaree.

5. And when I got home for supper, it was about half past nine;
   And when I had it ate well, I reckoned it was bedtime.
   The cocky he came over to me, and he said with a merry laugh,
   "I want you now for an hour or two to cut a bit of chaff."

6. And when I had it finished, I'd to nurse the youngest child;
   Whenever I said a joking word, the missus she would smile.
   The old fellow got jealous, looked like he'd murder me;
   And there he sat and whipped the cat, the cocky from Bungaree.

7. Well, when I had my first week done, I reckoned I'd had enough;
   I walked up to the cocky, and I asked him for my stuff.
   I went down in to Ballarat, and it didn't last me long;
   I went straight in to Sayer's Hotel, and I blew my one pound one.

The Wild Rover

The story of a young man reformed from drinking, this is quite a popular
song in Ireland, England, and Australia.

Adapted by Pat Clancy, Tom Clancy,
Liam Clancy, and Tommy Makem

I've been a wild ro - ver for man - y a year, _____ And I've
I went in - to an ale house I used to fre - quent, _____ And I

spent all my mon - ey on whis - key and beer. _____ But now I'm re -
told the land - la - dy my mon - ey was spent. _____ I asked for a

turn - ing with gold in great store, _____ And I nev - er will play the wild
bot - tle; she an - swered me "Nay, _____ Such a cus - tom as yours I can

3. Then out of my pocket I took sovereigns bright,
   And the landlady's eyes opened wide with delight.
   She said, "I have whiskies and wines of the best,
   And the words that I said, sure, were only in jest."
   Chorus

4. I'll go back to my parents, confess what I've done,
   And ask them to pardon their prodigal son.
   And if they caress me as oftimes before,
   Then I never will play the wild rover no more.
   Chorus

Fare Thee Well, Enniskillen

Irish men went off to fight in many wars, but no matter how much they enjoyed their travels in foreign lands, they were always happy to return home.

New words by Tommy Makem
Music traditional

1. Our troop was made read-y at the dawn of the day; From
2. Oh, Spain it is a gal-lant land where wine and ale flow free; There's

love-ly En-nis-kil-len they were march-ing us a-way. They put us then on
lots of love-ly wom-en there to dan-dle on your knee. And of-ten in a

board a ship to cross the rag-ing main, To fight in blood-y bat-tle in the
tav-ern there we'd make the raf-ters ring When ev-'ry sol-dier in the house would

sun - ny land of Spain. Fare thee well, En - nis - kil - len, fare thee well for a - while, And
raise his glass and sing.

all a - round the bor - ders of Er - in's green isle. And when the war is o - ver, we'll re-

turn in full bloom, And you'll all wel-come home the En - nis - kil - len___ Dra - goons.

3. Well, we fought for Ireland's glory there, and many a man did fall
   From musket and from bayonet and from thundering cannonball.
   And many a foeman we laid low amid the battle throng,
   And as we prepared for action you would often hear this song:
   Chorus

4. Well, now the fighting's over, and for home we have set sail;
   Our flag above this lofty ship is fluttering in the gale.
   They've given us a pension, boys, of fourpence each a day,
   And when we reach Enniskillen, nevermore we'll have to say:
   Chorus

Mick McGuire

The best known of Irish music-hall songs, this is about a young man with
mother-in-law trouble.

Adapted by Pat Clancy, Tom Clancy,
Liam Clancy, and Tommy Makem

1. Oh, me name is Mick Mc-Guire,__ and I'll quick-ly tell to you Of a
2. Now, the first time that I met her was at the dance at Tar-ma-gee, And I

young girl I ad-mired__ called__ Ka-ty Don-a-hue. She was
ver-y kind-ly asked her if she'd dance a step with me. Then I

fair and fat and for - ty, and be - lieve me when I say
asked if I could see her home, if I'd be go - ing her way,
That when-
And when-

ev - er I came in at the door you could hear her mam - my say:
ev - er I'd come in at the door you could hear her mam - my say:

"John - ny, get up from the fire; get up and give the man a sate. Can't you

see it's Mis - ter Mc - Guire,__ and he's court - ing your sis - ter Kate? Ah, you

know ver - y well he owns a farm a wee bit out of the town. Ar - ragh, get

up out of that, you im - pu - dent brat, and let Mis - ter Mc - Guire sit down."

Chorus

Did - dle e dow - dle - ow - dle - ow - dle, did - dle e dow - dle - ow - dle - ow, Did - dle e

dow - dle - ow - dle - ow - dle, did - dle e dow - dle - ow - dle - ow. "Ah, you

know ver - y well he owns that farm a wee bit out of the town. Ar - ragh, get

up out of that, you im - pu - dent brat, and let Mis - ter Mc - Guire sit down."

3. Ah, but now that we are married, shure, her mother's changed her mind,
Just because I spent the legacy her father left behind.
She hasn't got the decency to bid me time of day;
Now whenever I come in at the door you'd hear the auld one say:
"Johnny, come up to the fire, come up; you're sitting in a draft.
Can't you see it's auld McGuire, and he nearly drives me daft?
Ah, I don't know what gets into him, for he's always on the tare.
Arragh, just sit where you are and never you dare to give auld McGuire the chair."

Chorus:
Diddle e dowdle-owdle-owdle,
    diddle e dowdle-owdle-ow,
Diddle e dowdle-owdle-owdle,
    diddle e dowdle-owdle-ow.
"Ah, I don't know what gets into him,
    for he's always on the tare.
Arragh, just sit where you are and never you dare
    to give auld McGuire the chair."

Isn't It Grand, Boys?

This is an old English music-hall song.

Adapted by Pat Clancy, Tom Clancy,
Liam Clancy, and Tommy Makem

1. Look at the cof - fin_____ With gold - en han -
2. Look at the flow - ers_____ All blood - y - well with -

dles._____ Is - n't it grand, boys,_____ To be
ered._____ Is - n't it grand, boys,_____ To be

blood - y - well dead?_____ Let's not have a snif - fle;_____
blood - y - well dead?_____

Let's have a blood-y - good cry._____ And al - ways re - mem - ber: The

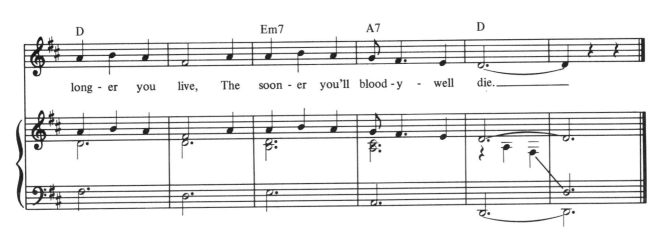

long - er you live, The soon - er you'll blood - y - well die._____

3. Look at the mourners,
   Bloody-great hypocrites.
   Isn't it grand, boys,
   To be bloody-well dead?
   Chorus

4. Look at the preacher,
   Bloody-nice fellow.
   Isn't it grand, boys,
   To be bloody-well dead?
   Chorus

5. Look at the widow,
   Bloody-great female.
   Isn't it grand, boys,
   To be bloody-well dead?
   Chorus

The Beggarman

Very often in folk music the life of the footloose wanderer is celebrated. The hero of this song is such a charming, happy fellow he could very easily make you hitch on your pack and follow him on the road.

Adapted by Sarah Makem

1. I am a lit - tle beg - gar - man and beg - ging I have been For
2. I slept in a barn down at Cur - ra - bawn; A

three score or more in this lit - tle isle of green; I'm known from the Lif - fey
wet night came on and I slept till the dawn, With holes in the roof and the

down to Se - gue, And I'm known by the name of old John - ny Dhu. Of
rain com - ing through And the rats and the cats, they were play - ing peek - a - boo. When

all the trades that's go - in' now, sure beg - gin' is the best; Ah for
who should a - wa - ken but the wo - man of the house, With her

when a man is tired, he can sit down and rest. Beg for his din - ner, he has
white spot - ty a - pron, her cal - i - co blouse; She be - gan to fright - en and

noth - ing else to do, On - ly cut a - round the cor - ner with his old rig - a - doo.
I said, "Boo! Ar - rah don't be a - fraid ma'am, it's on - ly John - ny Dhu."

Chorus
Hey! Did - dle - le die - dee doo die - dle - le dee - dle did - dle dum, Did - dle - le

doo-dle die-dle did-dle dad-dle did-dle die-dle dum. Di - doo-dle die-dle did-dle die-dle

did-dle - le die-dle dum, Did-dle - le doo-dle die-dle did-dle da-dle doom da - da.

3. I met a little flaxy-haired girl one day;
"Good morning, little flaxy-haired girl," I did say.
"Good morning, little beggarman, a-how do you do,
With your rags and your bags and your old rigadoo?"
"I'll buy a pair of leggings, a collar and a tie;
And a nice young lady I'll fetch bye and bye.
I'll buy a pair of goggles and colour them blue;
And an old-fashioned lady, I will make her too."
Chorus

4. Over the road with my pack on my back,
Over the fields with my great heavy sack,
With holes in my shoes and my toes peeping through,
Singing, "Skinny-ma-rink-a-doodle-o and old Johnny Dhu."
I must be going to bed, for it's getting late at night;
The fire's all raked and out goes the light.
So now you've heard the story of my old rigadoo;
"It's goodbye and God be with you," says old Johnny Dhu.
Chorus

Irish Rover

Of all the tall tales of tall ships, none had a cargo
to compare with the fabulous *Irish Rover*.

Adapted by Pat Clancy, Tom Clancy,
Liam Clancy, and Tommy Makem

Brightly, and with energy

1. In the year of our Lord eight - een hun - dred and six We set
2. There was Bar - ney Ma - gee, from the banks of the Lee; There was

sail from the coal quay of Cork, We were sail - ing a - way with a
Ho - gan, from Coun - ty Ty - rone. There was John - ny Mc-Gurk, who was

car - go of bricks For the grand cit - y hall in New York. We'd an
scared stiff of work, And a chap from West-meath named Ma - lone. There was

3. We had one million bags of the best Sligo rags,
   We had two million barrels of bone;
   We had three million bales of old nanny goats' tails,
   We had four million barrels of stone.
   We had five million hogs and six million dogs
   And seven million barrels of porter;
   We had eight million sides of old blind horses' hides
   In the hold of the *Irish Rover*.

4. We had sailed seven years when the measels broke out,
   And our ship lost her way in a fog.
   And the whole of the crew was reduced down to two;
   'Twas myself and the captain's old dog.
   Then the ship struck a rock, O Lord, what a shock,
   And nearly tumbled over;
   Turned nine times around, then the poor old dog was drowned.
   I'm the last of the *Irish Rover*.

170

Cruiscín Lán

(KROOSH-KEEN LAWN)

"Cruiscín Lán" means "Little Full Jug"; "grá mo chroi mó cruiscín": "love of my heart, my little jug"; "slainte geal mo mhuairnin": "bright health, my precious one." Poetically this is one of the better drinking songs. The music of the chorus sounds more German than Irish, but the sentiments are universal to any drinking man.

Adapted by Pat Clancy, Tom Clancy, Liam Clancy, and Tommy Makem

1. Let the farm-er praise his grounds, Let the hunts-man praise his hounds, Let the shep-herd praise his dew-y-scent-ed lawn._____ Oh, but I'm more wise than they, Spend each hap-py night and day With my dar-lin' lit-tle cruis-cín *kroosh-keen*

2. Im - mor-tal and di-vine, Great__ Bac-chus, god of wine,__ Cre-ate me by a-dop-tion your own son,_____ In hopes that you'll com-ply That my glass shall ne'er run dry Nor my dar-lin' lit-tle cruis-cín

3. Oh, when cruel death appears
   In a few but happy years,
   You'll say, "Oh, won't you come along with me?"
   I'll say, "Begone, you knave,
   For King Bacchus gave me lave
   To take another cruiscín lán, lán, lán,
   To take another cruiscín lán."
   Chorus

4. Then fill your glasses high;
   Let's not part with lips so dry,
   For the lark now proclaims it is the dawn.
   And since we can't remain,
   May we shortly meet again
   To fill another cruiscín lán, lán, lán,
   To fill another cruiscín lán.
   Chorus

Galway Races

All the noise and fun of the races—the sport of kings.

Adapted by Pat Clancy, Tom Clancy,
Liam Clancy, and Tommy Makem

1. As I rode down to Gal - way Town to seek for rec - re - a - tion On the
2. There were pas - sen - gers from Lim - er - ick and more from Tip - per - ar - y,___ The

sev - en - teen of Au - gust, my mind be - ing el - e - vat - ed, There was
boys from Con - ne - mar - a and the Clare un - mar - ried maid - ens, And

mul - ti - tudes as - sem - bled with their tick - ets at the sta - tion; Me
peo - ple from Cork Cit - y who were loy - al, true and faith - ful, They brought

eyes be - gan to daz - zle and they're go - in' to see the rac - es.
home the Fen - ian pris - on - ers from dy - ing in for - eign na - tions.

Chorus

With me whack fol the do fol the did - dle - ly id - le ay.

3. It's there you'll see confectioners with sugarsticks and dainties,
And lozenges and oranges and lemonade and raisins,
And gingerbread and spices to accomodate the ladies,
And a big crubeen for thruppence to be pickin' while you're able.
Chorus

4. It's there you'll see the pipers and the fiddlers competing,
The nimble-footed dancers, and they trippin' on the daisies,
And others cryin' cigars and lights and bills for all the races,
With the colours of the jockeys and the price and horses' ages.
Chorus

174

5. It's there you'll see the jockeys, and they mounted on so stately,
   The blue, the pink, the orange and green, the emblem of our nation.
   When the bell was rung for starting, all the horses seemed impatient;
   I thought they never stood on ground, their speed was so amazing.
   Chorus

6. There was half a million people there of all denominations,
   The Catholic, the Protestant, the Jew and Presbyterian;
   There was yet no animosity, no matter what persuasion,
   But fortune and hospitality inducing fresh acquaintance.
   Chorus

Portláirge

(PURTH-LAW-RIG-EH)

In Ireland people would gather in the pubs on fair days and market days
when their business of the day had ended, to "wet their whistle" and hear a
song. A traveling piper, fiddler, singer, or fluter would provide sweet music
for pennies, and a farmer could learn a new song or two. Our grandmother
kept one of these pubs and learned quite a few songs, one of which was
"Portláirge," a local Gaelic song. All the place names mentioned are within
twenty miles of her pub.

Adapted by Jack Keenan, Pat Clancy, Tom Clancy,
Liam Clancy, and Tommy Makem

1. Ó do bhios-sa lá i Port-láir - ge, Fol dow fol dee fol the dad eye um, Bhi—
Oh dhu vee - sah law Burth - law-rig-eh, Vee—

fion is punch ar chlár____ ann, Fol dow fol dee fol the dad eye um, Bhi
feen iss punch err klawr____ oun, *Vee*

lán á ti de mhńaibh ann, Fol dow fol dee fol the dad eye um, Ag - us
lawn ah tee dhe vnaw-iv oun, *Og-gus*

mise ag ól a sláin - te, Fol dow fol dee fol the dad eye um.
mish egg ohl ah slawn - teh,

2. Agus d'éaluigh bean ó Rath liom,
   Og-gus thale-ig ban oh Raw lum,

   Fol dow fol dee fol the dad eye um,

   Agus triúr ó Thiobraid Árann,
   Og-gus throor oh Hibb-ar-idh Awr-on,

   Fol dow fol dee fol the dad eye um,

   Ni raibh a muintir sásta,
   Nee rev ah mween-thar saws-tha,

   Fol dow fol dee fol the dad eye um,

   Ni rabhadar ach leath-shásta,
   Nee row-dhar ock lah-haws-tha,

   Fol dow fol dee fol the dad eye um.

3. Ó raghadsa ón Charraig amárach,
   Oh ride-sah oan Korr-igg am-awr-ock,

   Fol dow fol dee fol the dad eye um,

   Agus tabharfad cailin bréa liom,
   Og-gus thaur-hadh koll-een brah lum,

   Fol dow fol dee fol the dad eye um,

   Gabhfaimid trid an Bhearnan,
   Go-meedh treedh on Vaar-nan,

   Fol dow fol dee fol the dad eye um,

   Ó thuaidh go Thiobraid Árann,
   Oh how-ig guh Hibb-ar-idh Awr-on

   Fol dow fol dee fol the dad eye um.

Eamon de Valera.

Foggy Dew

This song of the Easter rising of 1916 was an appeal for Irishmen to die fighting for their own country rather than die in some foreign war in a British uniform. Suvla was a battleground in the Middle East. "Pearse" and "Valera," mentioned in the third stanza, refer to Patrick Pearse, leader of the Easter rising, and Eamon de Valera, who later became prime minister of Ireland.

Adapted by Pat Clancy, Tom Clancy,
Liam Clancy, and Tommy Makem

1. 'Twas down the glen one Easter morn To a cit - y fair rode
2. Right proud-ly high o - ver Dub-lin town They hung out a flag of

I, When Ire - land's lines of march - ing men In
war; 'Twas bet - ter to die 'neath an I - rish sky Than at

3. 'Twas England bade our wild geese go
   That small nations might be free;
   Their lonely graves are by Suvla's waves
   On the fringe of the grey North Sea.
   But had they died by Pearse's side
   Or fought with Valera true,
   Their graves we'd keep where the Fenians sleep,
   'Neath the hills of the foggy dew.

4. The bravest fell, and the solemn bell
   Rang mournfully and clear
   For those who died that Eastertide
   In the springing of the year.
   And the world did gaze in deep amaze
   At those fearless men and true
   Who bore the fight that freedom's light
   Might shine through the foggy dew.

The Parting Glass

A sentimental drinking song that closes the evening at many an Irish pub, "The Parting Glass" is the traditional farewell song of the Clancy family.

Adapted by Pat Clancy

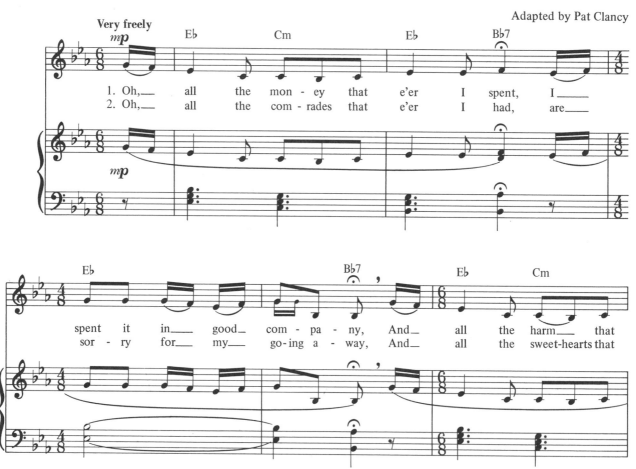

1. Oh,__ all the mon - ey that e'er I spent, I__ spent it in__ good__ com - pa - ny, And__ all the harm__ that
2. Oh,__ all the com - rades that e'er I had, are__ sor - ry for__ my__ go - ing a - way, And__ all the sweet-hearts that

184

Index of Recordings

Columbia CL 2165/*CS 8965*	**An Poc Ar Buile (50)**	The Clancy Brothers and Tommy Makem
Columbia CL 2265/*CS 9065*	**Ar Fol Lol Lol O (13)**	The Clancy Brothers and Tommy Makem
Columbia CL 1909/*CS 8709*	**As I Roved Out (44)**	The Clancy Brothers and Tommy Makem
Tradition 1044	**As I Roved Out**	Tommy Makem
Tradition 1034	**As I Roved Out**	Clancy Children
Columbia CS 9608	**The Bard of Armagh (56)**	The Clancy Brothers and Tommy Makem
Tradition 1042	**The Bard of Armagh**	The Clancy Brothers and Tommy Makem
Tradition 91182	**The Bard of Armagh**	The Clancy Brothers and Tommy Makem
Columbia CL 2265/*CS 9065*	**The Beggarman (164)**	The Clancy Brothers and Tommy Makem
Tradition 1044	**The Beggarman**	Tommy Makem
Columbia CS 9608	**The Black Cavalry (40)**	The Clancy Brothers and Tommy Makem
Columbia CL 2694/*CS 9494*	**Blackwater Side (92)**	The Clancy Brothers and Tommy Makem
Vanguard 9169	**Blackwater Side**	Liam Clancy
Tradition 1044	**Blow Ye Winds (68)**	Tommy Makem
Columbia CS 9805	**Bold Tenant Farmer (132)**	The Clancy Brothers and Tommy Makem
Tradition 1042	**Bold Tenant Farmer**	The Clancy Brothers and Tommy Makem
Tradition 91182	**Bold Tenant Farmer**	The Clancy Brothers and Tommy Makem
Tradition 1006	**Boulavogue (70)**	The Clancy Brothers and Tommy Makem
Tradition 1042	**Bungle Rye (100)**	The Clancy Brothers and Tommy Makem
Tradition 91182	**Bungle Rye**	The Clancy Brothers and Tommy Makem
Tradition 1045	**Bungle Rye**	Peg and Bobby Clancy
Columbia CL 2265/*CS 9065*	**The Butcher Boy (120)**	The Clancy Brothers and Tommy Makem
Tradition 1044	**The Butcher Boy**	Tommy Makem
Columbia CL 2477/*CS 9277*	**The Cobbler (116)**	The Clancy Brothers and Tommy Makem
Tradition 1045	**The Cobbler**	Peg and Bobby Clancy
Columbia CL 2694/*CS 9494*	**The Cockies of Bungaree (151)**	The Clancy Brothers and Tommy Makem
Vanguard 9169	**Convict of Clonmel (140)**	Liam Clancy
Tradition 1006	**The Croppy Boy (72)**	The Clancy Brothers and Tommy Makem
Tradition 1032	**Cruiscín Lán (171)**	The Clancy Brothers and Tommy Makem
Columbia CL 2265/*CS 9065*	**The Curlew's Song (90)**	The Clancy Brothers and Tommy Makem
Columbia CL 2745/*CS 9545*	**The Curlew's Song**	Tommy Makem
Tradition 1006	**Éamonn an Chnoic (20)**	The Clancy Brothers and Tommy Makem
	The Earl of Moray (114)	
Columbia CL 2477/*CS 9277*	**Eileen Aroon (42)**	The Clancy Brothers and Tommy Makem
Tradition 1042	**Eileen Aroon**	The Clancy Brothers and Tommy Makem
Columbia CL 2745/*CS 9545*	**Ever the Winds (52)**	Tommy Makem
Columbia CS 9805	**Fare Thee Well, Enniskillen (156)**	The Clancy Brothers and Tommy Makem
Columbia CL 2536/*CS 9336*	**Foggy Dew (180)**	The Clancy Brothers and Tommy Makem
Columbia 32 15 0001	**Foggy Dew**	The Clancy Brothers and Tommy Makem
Tradition 1006	**Foggy Dew**	The Clancy Brothers and Tommy Makem
Tradition 1044	**Foggy Dew**	Tommy Makem
Columbia CS 9608	**Four Green Fields (130)**	The Clancy Brothers and Tommy Makem
Columbia CS 9711	**Four Green Fields**	Tommy Makem
Columbia CL 2536/*CS 9336*	**Freedom's Sons (135)**	The Clancy Brothers and Tommy Makem
Columbia CL 2745/*CS 9545*	**Freedom's Sons**	Tommy Makem
Columbia CL 2477/*CS 9277*	**Galway City (28)**	The Clancy Brothers and Tommy Makem
Columbia CL 2477/*CS 9277*	**Galway Races (173)**	The Clancy Brothers and Tommy Makem
Vanguard 9169	**Galway Races**	Liam Clancy
Columbia CL 2536/*CS 9336*	**Hi for the Beggarman (4)**	The Clancy Brothers and Tommy Makem
Vanguard 9169	**Hi for the Beggarman**	Liam Clancy
Columbia CL 1909/*CS 8709*	**The Holy Ground (6)**	The Clancy Brothers and Tommy Makem
Columbia CS 9608	**I Once Loved a Lass (16)**	The Clancy Brothers and Tommy Makem
Columbia CL 2477/*CS 9277*	**Isn't It Grand, Boys? (162)**	The Clancy Brothers and Tommy Makem
Columbia 4-43548	**Isn't It Grand, Boys?**	The Clancy Brothers and Tommy Makem
Columbia CL 1771/*CS 8571*	**Irish Rover (168)**	The Clancy Brothers and Tommy Makem
Tradition 1044	**Irish Rover**	Tommy Makem
Tradition 1042	**Johnny, I Hardly Knew Ye (31)**	The Clancy Brothers and Tommy Makem

Stereophonic records are indicated by *italics*. The numbers in parentheses after the song titles indicate page numbers in this book.

	Johnny Is a Roving Blade (10)	
Columbia CL 2265/*CS 9065*	**Lament for Brendan Behan (58)**	The Clancy Brothers and Tommy Makem
Columbia CL 2165/*CS 8965*	**The Leaving of Liverpool (65)**	The Clancy Brothers and Tommy Makem
Columbia CL 2536/*CS 9336*	**Lord Nelson (118)**	The Clancy Brothers and Tommy Makem
	The Lough Neagh Fishers (109)	
Tradition 1044	**The Lowlands of Holland (104)**	Tommy Makem
Tradition 1045	**Maderine Rue (126)**	Peg and Bobby Clancy
Tradition 1034	**Maderine Rue**	Clancy Children
Columbia CL 2265/*CS 9065*	**Maid of Fife-E-O (112)**	The Clancy Brothers and Tommy Makem
Tradition 1042	**Maid of Fife-E-O**	The Clancy Brothers and Tommy Makem
Tradition 1032	**The Maid of the Sweet Brown Knowe (26)**	The Clancy Brothers and Tommy Makem
Columbia CL 1950/*CS 8750*	**A Man of Double Deed (78)**	The Clancy Brothers and Tommy Makem
Tradition 1034	**A Man of Double Deed**	Clancy Children
Columbia CL 2694/*CS 9494*	**Master McGrath (102)**	The Clancy Brothers and Tommy Makem
Columbia CL 1909/*CS 8709*	**McPherson's Lament (128)**	The Clancy Brothers and Tommy Makem
Columbia CL 2694/*CS 9494*	**Mick McGuire (158)**	The Clancy Brothers and Tommy Makem
Tradition 1032	**Mick McGuire**	The Clancy Brothers and Tommy Makem
Tradition 1044	**The Month of January (98)**	Tommy Makem
Columbia CL 1771/*CS 8571*	**Mr. Moses Ri-Tooral-i-ay (38)**	The Clancy Brothers and Tommy Makem
	Mrs. Rockett's Pub (74)	
Columbia CL 2477/*CS 9277*	**My Son Ted (34)**	The Clancy Brothers and Tommy Makem
Columbia 4-43548	**Nancy Whiskey (146)**	The Clancy Brothers and Tommy Makem
Columbia CL 2477/*CS 9277*	**Nancy Whiskey**	The Clancy Brothers and Tommy Makem
Tradition 1006	**Nell Flaherty's Drake (46)**	The Clancy Brothers and Tommy Makem
Columbia CL 2477/*CS 9277*	**O'Donnell Abú (142)**	The Clancy Brothers and Tommy Makem
Tradition 1006	**O'Donnell Abú**	The Clancy Brothers and Tommy Makem
Columbia CL 1648/*CS 8448*	**The Old Orange Flute (148)**	The Clancy Brothers and Tommy Makem
Columbia CL 1950/*CS 8750*	**Óró, Sé Do Bheatha 'Bhaile! (2)**	The Clancy Brothers and Tommy Makem
Columbia 35 15 0001	**Óró, Sé Do Bheatha 'Bhaile!**	The Clancy Brothers and Tommy Makem
Tradition 1034	**Óró, Sé Do Bheatha 'Bhaile!**	Clancy Children
Tradition 1042	**Paddy Doyle's Boots (23)**	The Clancy Brothers and Tommy Makem
Tradition 91182	**Paddy Doyle's Boots**	The Clancy Brothers and Tommy Makem
Tradition 1034	**Paper of Pins (80)**	Clancy Children
Columbia CL 1950/*CS 8750*	**The Parting Glass (182)**	The Clancy Brothers and Tommy Makem
Tradition 1032	**The Parting Glass**	The Clancy Brothers and Tommy Makem
Columbia CL 2536/*CS 9336*	**Portláirge (176)**	The Clancy Brothers and Tommy Makem
Tradition 1032	**Portláirge**	The Clancy Brothers and Tommy Makem
Columbia CL 2536/*CS 9336*	**The Rapparee (106)**	The Clancy Brothers and Tommy Makem
	Redmond O'Hanlon (18)	
Columbia CL 2265/*CS 9065*	**The Rocks of Bawn (124)**	The Clancy Brothers and Tommy Makem
Columbia CL 2165/*CS 8965*	**Rocky Road to Dublin (54)**	The Clancy Brothers and Tommy Makem
Vanguard 9169	**Rocky Road to Dublin**	Liam Clancy
Columbia CL 2745/*CS 9545*	**Sally-O (88)**	Tommy Makem
Columbia CL 1771/*CS 8571*	**The 23rd of June (144)**	The Clancy Brothers and Tommy Makem
Columbia CL 2265/*CS 9065*	**Weela Wallia (84)**	The Clancy Brothers and Tommy Makem
Columbia CL 2477/*CS 9277*	**What Would You Do If You Married a Soldier? (24)**	The Clancy Brothers and Tommy Makem
Columbia CL 1950/*CS 8750*	**When I Was Young (86)**	The Clancy Brothers and Tommy Makem
Tradition 1034	**When I Was Young**	Clancy Children
Columbia CL 1771/*CS 8571*	**Whiskey, You're the Devil (62)**	The Clancy Brothers and Tommy Makem
Tradition 1032	**Whiskey, You're the Devil**	The Clancy Brothers and Tommy Makem
Columbia CL 2265/*CS 9065*	**The Wild Rover (154)**	The Clancy Brothers and Tommy Makem
Columbia CL 2694/*CS 9494*	**William Bloat (36)**	The Clancy Brothers and Tommy Makem
Columbia CL 2694/*CS 9494*	**Winds of Morning (122)**	The Clancy Brothers and Tommy Makem
Columbia CL 2745/*CS 9545*	**Winds of Morning**	Tommy Makem
Tradition 1006	**The Wind That Shakes the Barley (138)**	The Clancy Brothers and Tommy Makem
Columbia CL 1950/*CS 8750*	**The Wren Song (82)**	The Clancy Brothers and Tommy Makem
Tradition 1034	**The Wren Song**	Clancy Children